Peter the Great

CRITICAL ISSUES IN WORLD
AND INTERNATIONAL HISTORY
Series Editor: Morris Rossabi

Peter the Great

Second Edition

Paul Bushkovitch

ROWMAN & LITTLEFIELD
Lanham • Boulder • New York • London

Published by Rowman & Littlefield
A wholly owned subsidiary of
The Rowman & Littlefield Publishing Group, Inc.
4501 Forbes Boulevard, Suite 200, Lanham, Maryland 20706
www.rowman.com

Unit A, Whitacre Mews, 26-34 Stannary Street, London SE11 4AB,
United Kingdom

British Library Cataloguing in Publication Information Available

Library of Congress Cataloging-in-Publication Data
Names: Bushkovitch, Paul, author.
Title: Peter the Great / Paul Bushkovitch.
Description: Second edition. | Lanham : Rowman & Littlefield, [2016]
  | Series: Critical issues in world and international history | Includes
  bibliographical references and index.
Identifiers: LCCN 2015043588 (print) | LCCN 2015043734 (ebook) |
  ISBN 9781442254619 (cloth : alkaline paper) | ISBN9781442254626
  (paperback : alkaline paper) | ISBN 9781442254633 (electronic)
Subjects: LCSH: Peter I, Emperor of Russia, 1672–1725. | Emperors
  Russia—Biography. | Russia—History—Peter I, 1689–1725.
Classification: LCC DK131 .B897 2016 (print) | LCC DK131 (ebook) |
  DDC 947/.05092—dc23
LC record available at http://lccn.loc.gov/2015043588

Printed in the United States of America

Contents

Chronology

Introduction

In thirty-six years (1689–1725) as the ruler of Russia, Peter the Great transformed his country, reorganizing and strengthening the state and army, conquering new territories, and building a navy, a seaport, and a new capital in St. Petersburg. Perhaps most important, he Europeanized Russian culture, laying the foundations for the introduction into Russia of Western literature, science, and social and political thought. Later Russian history is not comprehensible without Peter, for it was his importation of European culture that made possible reform, liberalism, Western-style nationalism, and communism.

Peter did not do all this alone. He inherited a political and social system that put at the summit of wealth and power a land and serf-owning aristocracy, the boyars, who administered the state, commanded the army, and made politics under the firm leadership of the tsar. Peter's attempts to transform Russia necessarily involved the aristocracy, as there were no other social groups numerous and capable enough to help carry out the task. Yet this aristocracy was not altogether enthusiastic about Peter's policies. As we shall see, they were less conservative culturally than often portrayed, but unfavorable to many of Peter's political aims. The politics of Peter's reign were thus a continuous tug-of-war between the tsar and the aristocrats, a tug-of-war that Peter ultimately won. How he did it is the subject of this book.

Until recently historians of Russia had little to say about social elites. The reasons go deep into the nineteenth century, to the first Russian historians who worked from a thorough knowledge of sources, not merely from romantic legends. These were the historians of the "state" or "juridical" school, principally S. M. Solov'ev (1820–1879). The school was well named, for their history of Russia was the history of the state, which they understood to mean the history of its formal institutions and the policy of the tsar, the theoretical source of law and policy. The state school historians produced many studies of the institutions of Russia before and during Peter's reign, the Boyar Duma, the Senate, provincial administration, but all of these pioneering works had little to say about the men who ran these institutions. The tsar himself was an abstraction, the source of law, and as such, by definition all-powerful. They followed the development of legislation, which to them meant simply the evolving will of the tsar, much more rarely the implementation of law. The state school was not interested in the informal structures of power, which they saw as mere abuses of legality. Their account of the relations of the state to the aristocracy stressed the legal obligation to serve the state. When Solov'ev and others occasionally did turn their attention to the men who served Peter, they emphasized the role of talented plebeians like Alexander Menshikov or Pavel Iaguzhinskii rather than aristocrats like Fyodor Golovin, Boris Sheremetev, or the Princes Dolgorukii. The talented plebeians fitted better with the image of a law-based, bureaucratic state striving toward meritocracy.

Their studies had a political message, for like the founder of the school, B. N. Chicherin (1828–1904), these historians were mostly moderate liberals. They believed that nineteenth-century Russia was too immature for a constitution, but they greeted with enthusiasm the reforms of the 1860s, the abolition of serfdom, the creation of a modern judiciary, and modest elected local government, the zemstvos. In their view these reforms strengthened the legal basis of the state and on such a state based on law later generations could build a constitution. They saw Peter's reforms as the first crucial step in the direction of a law-based state. The result was a thorough study of policy and institutions, but also a history without people. The state school ignored the men (and sometimes women) who were politically important in Peter's time, leaving them to journalists, antiquarians, and genealogists. Later historians, like P. N. Miliukov (1859–1943), who also served as the leader of Russia's liberals, introduced the theme of the interaction of the state and society, but their view of the state was essentially Solov'ev's.

The fate of Russia after the October Revolution of 1917 paradoxically did little to change this picture. In theory, Marxism should lead the historian to more intense study of economy and society, including ruling classes. In the Soviet Union, however, theoretical Marxism soon gave way to the political needs of the moment. Soviet historians were encouraged to find in Peter's reforms a precedent for the state-led industrialization and modernization aspects of Soviet policy. In Joseph Stalin's time the study of earlier Russian social elites was positively dangerous for historians to pursue, for it was seen as a rival to the endless chronicle of rural and urban rebellion that was the officially sponsored task of the scholar. In the West, the Russian émigré historians inherited the ideals of the state school and passed them on to the first generations of Western historians of Russia. Once again, institutional change was the preferred theme, and it remained so into the 1970s.

The past decades have seen new ways of looking at earlier Russian history emerge in both Russia and the West. They emerged as a complicated interaction of two historiographic traditions, Russian and Western, both trying to overcome the earlier paradigms, and both with (quite different) political problems to deal with.

In the Soviet Union in the 1950s, historians began to cautiously challenge the inherited stereotypes, though mostly with regard to the sixteenth century, not Peter's time. The posthumous publications of the work of S. B. Veselovskii, a prerevolutionary historian who remained in the USSR and studied the history and functions of the boyar elite, stimulated interest in that area. A. A. Zimin and R. G. Skrynnikov both produced different accounts of the events of the sixteenth century that had this in common—that they paid detailed attention to the interaction of the tsar and the boyars. In the process they also were able to map out the composition of the boyar elite and note its role in politics. Politically their work was in large part a response to the Stalin era, and as a result they devoted disproportionate attention to the Oprichnina period of the reign of Ivan the Terrible, and described it in excessively modern terms. On the other hand, they and their students transformed our knowledge and understanding of the sixteenth century.

In the West, politics of the Cold War era were intertwined with the traditions of the state school to produce extravagant claims for the power and effectiveness of the Russian state in the centuries before Peter. The Russian state became a proto-totalitarian dictatorship, the tsars masters over cowering slaves who possessed not even a will of their own. In reaction to these anachronistic conceptions, American historians of Russia in particular began to examine the actual structure of the state and its personnel. Basing themselves on the work of Gustave Alef as well as that of Zimin and Skrynnikov, Nancy Kollmann and Robert Crummey examined the boyar elite of the sixteenth and seventeenth centuries, while John LeDonne took on Peter's time and the eighteenth century. Though they all see things somewhat differently, all three agreed that the traditional Western view of the Russian state was a vast exaggeration and that the tsar's theoretical power was in reality exercised in concert with an old, established, wealthy, powerful, and self-conscious elite, the boyars. The informal power of this elite continued through Peter's reign and to the end of the eighteenth century, broken only by the creation of modern bureaucracy in the nineteenth century.

The Russian elite, LeDonne and his colleagues argue, was organized less by individual families than by clans. In the time before Peter, these clans operated as units to maintain their rank and power in the Boyar Duma, the administration, and the army. The formal structure of the Duma and the precedence system allowed them to do that. After Peter's death, his attempt to professionalize the state and army through the Table of Ranks was only a partial success. At the summit of power, the great clans continued to divide up the spoils of power and office in a complex process of negotiation with the tsars. The resulting picture is of a state much less "modern," less bureaucratic than that portrayed by earlier historians. This discussion has to a large extent replicated recent thinking about the early modern state in Western Europe. Until the 1960s, most historians stressed the modernity of the early modern state (Geoffrey Elton for England, for example), while more recent scholarship has tended in the opposite direction, to emphasize the archaic, prebureaucratic features of the state (William Beik and others for France).

Little of the reevaluation of the Russian state has so far reached the era of Peter the Great. LeDonne's account of the elite of that period is the only attempt to do so hitherto. He has stressed not only the continuity of the elite, but also the crucial importance of the alliance of the great families with the relatives of the tsar, the Saltykovs and the Naryshkins, the families of Peter's sister-in-law (the wife of his half-brother Ivan) and of his mother, Natalia Naryshkina. Like Kollmann and Crummey, LeDonne shares the presumption that the clans were the organizing unit of boyar society and thus generally united in their efforts to preserve their position in politics.

LeDonne is certainly right to stress the central importance of the clans whose women married into the ruling dynasty. However, it seems forced to group the ruling elite around those families. As Crummey has pointed out, the factions at court were not stable over decades, while the families were. More generally, the aristocratic clan may have been deeply concerned that all its men receive important positions, but the members did not always agree on political issues. We shall see important examples of divided clans.

How are we to better understand Russian politics in Peter's time? The scene of political action was the court, for formal institutions like the Boyar Duma and the Senate were composed of great aristocrats who were also part of the tsar's court, as in the West. At the time, Russians, foreign observers, and diplomats thought of the court as the central unit embracing the monarch and the political elite. (I am using the term "court" in the general sense of any monarch's court, not in the specific pre-Peter Russian sense of the "sovereign's court" [*gosudarev dvor*], meaning the household, the Duma ranks, and the upper military and administrative cadre, almost all of them landholders.) The court involved not merely the formal institutions of government, but the informal networks of family, friendship, favoritism, and patronage that bound up the elite in a tangled web of alliances and rivalries. These networks of formal and informal power formed the inner structure of Russian politics, and we can understand events only by keeping these networks in mind. Formal changes in administration, like the establishment of the Senate or the Colleges, should be understood not just as matters of administrative efficiency or Western influence, but also in reference to the personnel that manned them and their informal networks.

The networks add one new dimension to the known formal structures. Another is the assumptions in the minds of the men who staffed them on the eve of Peter's reign and during it. These assumptions were not complex intellectual systems derived from reading. The Russian aristocrats of Peter's time, even the best educated, were neither intellectuals nor ideologists; they were practical men of action. They did, however, have opinions about politics, religion, and particularly Peter's concrete policies. They inherited from their ancestors a conception of the rules of the game, so to speak, in Russian politics. In their minds, the rules of the game implied that the tsar should consult and respect them, promote them to high office, but not favor one of them over the others or over any nonaristocratic favorite (like Menshikov). Peter, like his father, agreed with most of this, except that he felt fully justified in promoting his favorites (and other nonaristocratic Russians or foreigners of merit). The aristocrats saw their mutual rivalries as justified to maintain their position, and had no qualms about complaining about Peter or even resisting him, if they could find a legitimate alternative, like Peter's son Aleksei. Peter saw both the aristocratic rivalries and resistance to his rule as disloyalty. How Peter and the aristocrats managed with these differences is one of the main subjects of this book.

Besides basic assumptions about political behavior, the rules of the game, Peter and the boyars inherited a very traditional conception of what we call politics, essentially a religious and moral view of how the tsar ought to behave, and how the boyars and people should react to his behavior. They did not conceive of any of this in terms we would call political, for our conception, since the Renaissance, is essentially secular, not religious. Russians did not know and were not interested in Western political thought before Peter. During his reign, however, that changed. As Russians, mainly noblemen at first, began to travel in Europe, learn Western languages, and read Western books, they began to familiarize themselves with a whole new vocabulary of politics and the theories it reflected. By the end of Peter's reign, notions of European monarchy and state sovereignty began to replace Russian tradition in the mind of Peter and his supporters. His aristocratic opponents began to create aristocratic notions, in part based on a mythical golden age of the great families under Tsar Aleksei. These changes in political thought were dependent both on larger changes in Russian culture and on the political history of Peter's reign, a complicated and shifting story.

All these elements come together to account for the character and success of Peter's reforms. There is much to Peter's reign that is not touched upon here. Foreign policy plays a subordinate role. Many of the changes in Russian culture, including religion, can only be dealt with very superficially. The economic basis of aristocratic wealth is poorly known for this period, and the economics of the Russian state only imperfectly. Popular reactions to Peter's reign play no role here, though we can get a glimpse of some aspects of those reactions. It is very difficult to evaluate the importance of those popular reactions: We know mostly about the hostility to his cultural reforms in the early part of the reign, for after 1708 there were few rebellions and the later personal or local instances of dissent are not necessarily representative. It is unclear what impact, if any, the popular reaction to Peter (even if as hostile as usually depicted) had on his policies. All these issues are beyond our scope, and most need much further research if we are to make sense of them.

Peter and the boyar aristocracy were the only forces of any power in Russian society in 1700, and it is their interaction that determined the fate of his reforms.

FURTHER READING

Hughes, Lindsey. *Russia in the Age of Peter the Great*. New Haven, CT: Yale University Press, 1998.

LeDonne, John P. "Ruling Families in the Russian Political Order 1689–1825," *Cahiers du Monde russe et sovietique* XXVIII, nos. 3–4 (1987): 233–322.

Riasanovsky, Nicholas V. *The Image of Peter the Great in Russian History and Thought*. New York: Oxford University Press, 1985.

Solov'ev, S. M. *Istoriia Rossii s drevneishikhvremen*, 26 volumes, Moscow 1960–66 (originally 1851–79). Available in English as Sergei M. Soloviev, *History of Russia*, 9 vols. Gulf Breeze, FL: Academic International Press, 1976–.

Wittram, Reinhard. *Peter der Grosse: Czar und Kaiser*, vols. 1–2. Göttingen: Vandenhoeck and Ruprecht, 1964 (best on Peter in any language).

For some comparative framework showing the evolution of ideas on the state in early modern Western Europe, see

Beik, William. *Absolutism and Society in Seventeenth-Century France: State Power and Provincial Aristocracy in Languedoc*. Cambridge, UK: Cambridge University Press, 1985.

Collins, James B. *The State in Early Modern France*. Cambridge, UK: Cambridge University Press, 2009.

Elton, Geoffrey. *The Tudor Revolution in Government: Administrative Changes in the Reign of Henry VIII*. Cambridge, UK: Cambridge University Press, 1953.

Chapter One

Russia at the End of the Seventeenth Century

Peter the Great inherited a country with long and complex political and cultural traditions. The deeper layers of Russian history went back to the ninth century, though the specific political and social structure of Peter's youth had been formed only about two hundred years before. All of this history was part of the intellectual equipment of the reformer tsar and the elite with which he worked and often struggled.

RUSSIAN ORIGINS

Russia was the largest of the states to emerge on the eastern periphery of Europe at the end of the Middle Ages. A state that we may call "Russia" came into being at the very end of the fifteenth century, under the rule of the Grand Princes of Moscow. The formation of Russia was the culmination of two centuries of struggle by the Moscow princes to achieve control of the surrounding territory, but if we must name a precise moment, then the best is the year 1478. In that year Ivan III (1462–1505) of Moscow finally incorporated the republic of Novgorod into his lands, thus uniting the two principal centers of medieval Russia, Moscow and Novgorod.

The Russia that emerged at the end of the fifteenth century was a new state, but not a new people. The Russian people, together with the Belorussians and Ukrainians, are the descendants of the population of the early medieval society known as Kievan Rus', an East Slavic state that came into being in the ninth century around the towns of Kiev and Novgorod. The rulers of Kiev Rus' sprang from the dynasty of the legendary Viking Riurik, who supposedly came to Novgorod to rule in 862. His descendants came to rule a vast territory, comprising the core of the modern states of Russia, Belarus' (Belorussia), and the Ukraine. Today the peoples of these states speak closely related languages that form the eastern group of the Slavic languages, but in Kievan times, there was only one language common to all. There was also one state, a loose confederation of local dynasties of Riurikovich princes, with the eldest branch of the dynasty ruling in Kiev. The most important feature of Kievan culture was the adoption of Christianity by Prince Vladimir Sviatoslavich in 988. Vladimir adopted Orthodox Christianity from the Byzantine Empire of the Greeks, putting his people into a different cultural world from that of Latin Western Europe. The adoption of Orthodox Christianity had profound effects, but for the moment the most important was the creation of an East Slavic literary language. In the West, the Roman church required the use of Latin as a liturgical language, making Latin the language of culture throughout Western Europe. The Greek church, in contrast, did not require Greek, so the new Christians of Russia (and the Balkans) came to use a Slavic liturgical language very close to the speech of the people of Kiev Rus'. Thus the eastern Slavs came to write in a language very close to their spoken dialects from the very beginning of Christianization. At the same time, the lack of Greek meant that they had little contact with Byzantine high culture and the works of classical antiquity.

The Kievan Rus' state came to an end in the thirteenth century. Internal dissension had led to decentralization and mutual warfare among the princes, but the end came with the Mongol conquest of 1237–40. Batu Khan, the grandson of Genghis Khan, led a Mongol army west across the inner Asian steppes to capture and destroy Kiev and other centers. He marched on westward into Central Europe, but the death of the ruling khan back in Mongolia put an end to further efforts at conquest in the west. Most of Kiev Rus', however, remained under the control of Batu and his successors. His followers set up a nomadic state (the "Golden Horde") based in the lower valley of the Volga River, a state whose people were mostly Turkic in speech rather than Mongol, and who ruled the territories of the former Kiev Rus' as vassal states of the khan. The dependent territories included all of the core of the future Russia—Novgorod, Vladimir, Moscow.

Under Mongol rule the territories in the northeast of Kiev Rus' gradually formed a center around the town and principality of Vladimir, northeast of Moscow. Already a major center in the twelfth century, Vladimir came to dominate the area. The Grand Prince of Vladimir, Alexander Nevskii (c. 1220–1263), not only ruled Vladimir but had been elected prince of Novgorod, where his defeat of the Swedes in 1240 at the Neva River earned him the nickname "Nevskii."[1] Alexander did not try to fight the Golden Horde, which was far too powerful at that time, and even went to Mongolia on the khan's insistence. Alexander's successors in Moscow struggled with the rival principality of Tver' throughout the fourteenth century for supremacy in the area, using the khans of the Golden Horde to destroy their enemies and building coalitions among the Russian princes. By the end of the century it was clear that Moscow had won. It helped the Moscow princes that the church early on threw its support to Moscow.

At the same time, a new power arose in Lithuania under the native princes. The Lithuanian princes expanded into Belorussia and on south to the Ukraine. By 1400, Lithuania, under the Gediminovich dynasty, was one of the largest states in Europe (in area, not in population), a rival to Moscow and the Golden

Horde. In the centuries after the Mongol conquest, the various
eastern Slavic dialects began to move apart, forming the ancestors
of the modern Russian, Ukrainian, and Belorussian languages.
The adoption of Catholic Christianity by Lithuanian Prince Ja-
giello in 1386 created a hybrid society in the Lithuanian state.
Ethnic Lithuanians became Catholics, but the Belorussians and
Ukrainians remained Orthodox. To complicate matters, many of
the Lithuanian princes and nobles who settled among their eastern Slavic subjects became and remained Orthodox. The official
language of court and administration was an eastern Slavic dialect
based on Ukrainian and Belorussian, not Lithuanian. This was a
cultural situation of exceptional complexity.

The Russia that emerged in these centuries, in contrast, was a
much more homogeneous society. Ethnically, it was overwhelmingly Russian and Orthodox, although in the northwest and north
there were many Finnic-speaking people who had occupied the
land before the arrival of the Slavs in the ninth to eleventh centuries. The most important of these were the Karelians on the Finnish border, who had been part of medieval Novgorod and were
Orthodox in faith though Finnish in language. The geography of
Russia in 1500 was more complex than its ethnic composition.
Though the whole of the Russian territory at that time was a flat
plain (the Ural Mountains formed the eastern boundary), its land
was not uniform. The basis of Russian geography was a series
of ecological belts running roughly from west to east. Starting
with the north, the first is the tundra, a treeless plain above the
Arctic Circle populated by the nomadic Lapps (Saami) and other
peoples. At this early date, few Russians ventured so far north.
South of the tundra is the taiga, a broad belt of evergreen forests
running from central Finland east to the eastern shores of Siberia.
Too cold and with too short a growing season for extensive agriculture, the taiga was thinly populated with only small numbers of
Russians and Finns clustered along lake shores and river valleys.
South of the taiga, in a broad belt running from Estonia to Poland

in the west and narrowing eastward toward the Urals, is the forest zone. This zone in turn has many local variants, but generally speaking it was then heavily forested with a mixture of deciduous and evergreen trees and with many open spaces, especially in the southern parts. The soil here is thin and relatively poor, but in certain areas, around Moscow, Rostov, and other towns, suitable for agriculture. Russian society and the Russian state came into existence in this forest zone, in the open fields and clearings among the forests.

South of the forest zone is the steppe, not yet part of Russia but crucial to its fate. The steppe lands were open plains covered with high grass, much as Kansas was before the white men came. The steppe grass in the summer was so high it was said that a man on horseback could hide in it, and (again like Kansas) it was thick with wild animals of every sort. On the steppe since the third millennium B.C. a succession of nomadic peoples had formed a series of societies, the Iranian Scythians and Sarmatians, contemporaries of the ancient Greeks and Romans, and then the Huns, who challenged Rome itself from the steppe. After the Huns came Turkic peoples, the Khazars, Pechenegs, Cumans, and finally the Golden Horde. For the steppe peoples, Kievan Rus' and later on Lithuania and Russia were places of secondary concern, the objects of slave raids and tribute. The steppe south of Russia was merely a small part of the great Eurasian plain, running from Hungary in the west through present-day Rumania, Ukraine, Russia, and Kazakhstan east to Sinkiang, Mongolia, and Manchuria into northern China. For the steppe peoples like the Golden Horde, the rise and fall of empires in Central Asia and China was much more important than the forest lands to the north.

The preoccupation of the Golden Horde with other nomadic empires to the east and southeast meant that its control of Russia was distant and soon confined to the collecting of tribute. The adoption of Islam by the Golden Horde under Khan Uzbek in the 1340s put a further barrier between Russia and the Horde, though there was no attempt to Islamize the Russians. The Russians were first able to defeat the Horde in battle at Kulikovo in 1380, and soon after Central Asian rivals (Tamerlane) and internal dissensions caused it to split into several competing Tatar Khanates. These were the Kazan' Khanate on the middle Volga, Crimea, the Great Horde on the lower Volga, and the Nogais in northwest Kazakhstan, east of the lower Volga. Thus by the 1480s the successor states of the Horde were no longer a threat, and the Russian princes began to move against the Khanate of Kazan'.

The society and state of Russia in 1500 was equally uncomplicated. The country was largely rural and agrarian, with a thin population concentrated in the more fertile areas. Russian peasants were juridically free, not yet serfs. Many of them were still tenants of the crown, required only to pay taxes and to be judged by the prince's officials. Perhaps as many as a third were tenants of the church, mainly of the great monasteries, and many more were tenants of the landholding class. Moscow, Novgorod, and Pskov were major towns and increasingly important commercial centers, but the towns also harbored much of the landholding class. Moscow was the center for the prince's officials and soldiers. Most of the landholding class also served in the prince's army, forming the lightly armed cavalry that was the bulk of that force. The Russian army needed above all to fight the Tatars, and infantry was as yet useless to meet the skilled horsemen of the steppe.

At the local level, Russian government and administration was incredibly simple. Greater and lesser landholders supported by a few clerks and soldiers administered the provinces, each man having vast territories under his theoretical control. The governors of the major border fortresses like Novgorod were invariably of boyar rank and only they had a somewhat larger civil staff and real armed force. All of these local administrators were rewarded by the "feeding" (*kormlenie*) system, in which the local population literally provided the official with food and some cash according to a traditional order. Taxation, justice, and institutional structures were much simpler than in Western Europe. There was no learned legal profession, no Code of Justinian, only the oral tradition of the peasantry and the very modest collections of laws promulgated by the princes of Moscow.

Central government was only a bit more complicated. At the core of the government was the Grand Prince of Moscow with his household and court. The Grand Prince of Moscow had acquired his title in the fourteenth century, and by 1500 he increasingly styled himself Grand Prince of All Russia (Rus'). He was proud of his descent from the Riurikovich princes of Kiev and from the later princes of Vladimir. Prince Alexander Nevskii was his most famous ancestor. Ivan III increased his prestige in the world in 1472 when he married Sophia Paleologue, a Greek princess descended from the last Byzantine emperors, and further in 1480 when the last vestiges of Tatar rule disappeared. To demonstrate his great status, Ivan III began to cautiously title himself "tsar" in informal situations, rather than just Grand Prince. These were grand claims, but historians differ about the extent of real power on the part of the princes. Much of the problem comes from the paucity of relevant sources. There are no extant records of decision making, only documents recording the outcome and laconic comments in the chronicles. We can only judge the extent of princely power from the results. In the short run, the Grand Princes were certainly very powerful. They could exile any of the prominent aristocrats without any legal barrier, for Russia lacked a written legal culture that went beyond elementary property cases and criminal law. Custom gave the prince apparently unlimited power, but, as we shall see, it also prescribed strict limits to the prince's power of appointment and promotion. Exiled families rarely stayed out of power: If one generation never made it back to the Kremlin, the next usually did. In the long run, the result was a remarkable continuity in the composition of the Russian ruling elite. The old boyar families who served the Moscow princes in

the fourteenth century were still at the pinnacle of power throughout the sixteenth and seventeenth centuries. At their side were the
many princely families who had been there almost as long.

The household of the Grand Prince centered on the palace in
the Kremlin, from which he ruled Russia and ran his personal
estates. Around the Grand Prince was his court (*dvor*), several
hundred men at that time, bodyguards, courtiers, and household
administrators who acted as a sort of reserve for civil and military appointments. Much of the day-to-day management of the
court fell to the Grand Prince's major domo (*dvoretskii*), who
was a crucial figure in both the prince's household and the state.
The major domo sometimes was a boyar and sometimes not, but
in either case was at the head of the *dvor*. Finally, the treasury
(*kazna*) emerged from the household administration at the end of
the fifteenth century to become the single most important office
of state. From the 1480s until the middle of the sixteenth century
it was the preserve of two Greek families, the Khovrins from the
Crimea and later the Tarkhaniotes from the entourage of Sophia
Paleologue. The treasury kept the money, accounts, jewels, and
furs of the prince and oversaw the revenues of the state. It also
kept the records of foreign affairs, the copies of treaties, and the
enormously detailed accounts of negotiations with foreign po-
tentates that characterized the records of Russian foreign policy.
As opposed to the major domo and treasurer, the equerry (*koni-
ushii*) was always a boyar and was equally important to both the
prince's household and governing circles in general. Around 1500
the equerry usually came from the Cheliadnin clan, old Moscow
boyars who had served the prince since early in the fourteenth
century.

The equerry and sometimes the major domo and treasurer
formed the link of the household and court with the Boyar Duma.
Strictly speaking, the term "Boyar Duma" is the invention of later
historians. Sources of the fifteenth through seventeenth centuries
referred to it simply as "the boyars" or "the Duma," never the two

terms together, but we will keep to the modern tradition. Around 1500 the Boyar Duma was small, only ten to twelve men with the rank of boyar and some five to six with the untranslatable title *okol'nichii*, a sort of junior boyar. The men of boyar rank came from two groups. One was the Moscow elite of the fourteenth century, families like Morozov and Zakhar'ev-Iur'ev (Romanov). The other group was the princes, either descended from Riurik like the Grand Prince himself or from Gedimin, the prince of Lithuania. The princes had mostly been the rulers of small sovereign territories, either around Moscow or on the Lithuanian–Russian border and had come to serve the Moscow princes. Some, especially the border princes, had retained some autonomy for a time, but by 1500 such arrangements were nearly extinct. The *okol'nichii* generally came from lesser families of the same type of origin or from junior members of the great clans.

The order of precedence in the Boyar Duma, the appointments to the Duma, and the hierarchy of military and civil offices were all regulated by the precedence system, *mestnichestvo* in Russian. The precedence system, simply stated, meant that a given individual derived his offices from the rank of the offices held by his ancestors and by the overall distinction of the clan. The rules of precedence were not written down, but everyone knew them and could cite them in lawsuits. What the prince's clerks did write down were the names of the holders of offices and military commands, a new list every year, even if most of the names were the same. From the middle of the sixteenth century the clerks also began to compile an official Book of Genealogy. In theory, the genealogy and service lists would allow everyone to know precisely who could hold what office or command at any given time. In practice the complexities of the system led to many disputes, and especially for the army it was clumsy, leading the prince to override the system on campaign and move some new men up the ladder. The overall result was that the Grand Prince was not completely free to appoint whom he wished to the Duma or other offices. The clans eligible for the Duma were a known quantity, and within the clan the prince was supposed to appoint the elder males. The system did not prescribe a particular man for a specific office, only that no one of lower rank than a particular person could hold a higher-ranking position.

One factor that immensely complicated the calculations was the absence of primogeniture, the system of inheritance in which titles and property passed to the eldest son. In Russia, all the sons and daughters of a prince received the title. All were also entitled to a share of the property (even the daughters), though the practice was to reserve a somewhat larger or more important portion for the eldest male. The right to rank in the precedence system was similar: In theory all the sons of a boyar could become boyars.

Fortunately for the Grand Prince, custom did not dictate that he appoint all sons to the Duma when a boyar died. Further, the prince would often promote the dead man's brother to the Duma rather than his firstborn son, particularly if the son was still comparatively young. Sometimes the prince would appoint a young aristocrat to the lesser Duma rank of *okol'nichii*, a term signifying that lesser rank. Some men also stayed at the rank of *okol'nichii* all their lives. Finally, the conditions of life in the sixteenth century, especially for an elite that regularly fought in wars, meant that a man was unlikely to have more than two or three surviving sons at his death, and often fewer. Thus the Duma grew only very slowly as new appointments led to a gradual increase in the number of boyars in the Duma, up to some twenty by 1600, with a similar increase in lesser Duma ranks.

SIXTEENTH-CENTURY POLITICS

The politics of the Duma around 1500 are very difficult to penetrate. The reason is that almost all we know comes from a series of Russian chronicles, laconic in their manner of narration of events and mostly composed to defend the actions of Ivan III and his successors. It seems that for much of the second half of the fifteenth century the predominant group among the boyars was that of the Princes Patrikeev, descendants of one of the Lithuanian Gediminovichi who came to serve the Moscow princes in 1408. In the 1490s, however, the dominance of the Princes Patrikeev came to an end. It seems that they had supported the succession to the throne of Ivan III's grandson Dmitrii, whose father, Ivan III's eldest son by his first wife, had died. For reasons unclear to us Ivan III decided to leave his throne to Vasilii Ivanovich, the eldest son of his second wife, Sophia.

Prince Ivan Patrikeev and his two sons were sent into exile, and forcibly tonsured as monks in 1499. Their estates were confiscated and Ivan Patrikeev's son-in-law, Prince Semen Riapolovskii, was executed. As far as we can tell, it seems that the Patrikeevs had become too powerful for Ivan as well as for the other boyars, and their support for Dmitrii became the occasion of their removal. The fall of the Patrikeevs was the first of a series of boyar intrigues and conflicts with the ruler that occurred with increasing frequency throughout the sixteenth century.

Another player of importance in the political game was the church. The Orthodox Church in Russia had come into being in Kievan times as part of the universal Orthodox Church in Byzantium. Originally the heads of the Russian Church, with the title of metropolitan of Kiev, were appointed and sent from Constantinople. In the fifteenth century the rise of Lithuania led to a division of the church, with the metropolitan of Kiev coming under the rule of the Grand Princes of Lithuania and the rest under the metropolitan of Moscow. In 1441 the Russians expelled the Greek Metropolitan of Moscow Isidore, who had supported the union with the Catholic Church at the Council of Florence (1439). The Grand Prince of Moscow and the Russian bishops then in 1448 elected their own metropolitan, Iov, with the result that the church in Russia became in fact independent of Constantinople even before it fell to the Turks in 1453.

The metropolitans of Moscow and the hegumens (abbots) of the great monasteries in Russia were powerful figures. They were extremely wealthy, for they owned nearly a third of the cultivated land in the country. They were inevitably drawn into court politics, like the unfortunate Metropolitan Daniil, who was deposed (1539) by the boyar regency. Metropolitan Makarii, who moved from the see of Novgorod to the metropolitanate in 1542, was one of the dominant figures at the court of Ivan the Terrible until the metropolitan's death in 1563. In turn the princes and boyars were involved in the internal disputes in the church, like the one over the proper character and scale of monastic landholding that lasted from about 1500 through the 1530s. The leader of those monks who wanted restrictions on monastic landholding was Vassian Patrikeev, one of the younger Patrikeev princes who had been forcibly tonsured in 1499.

The intrigues among the boyars lasted through the reign of Vasilii III (1505–1533); on his death they exploded in murderous rivalries. His son Ivan, the future Ivan IV (the Terrible), was only three years old, and the result was a regency lasting until 1547. The years of the regency saw the Princes Shuiskii and Obolenskii in violent contention for power, each group trying to control the government and executing and exiling its opponents when in power. All this came to an end with the accession of Ivan IV in 1547, the first Russian ruler to be crowned tsar. The title signified his claim to equality in rank with the Byzantine emperors, the Holy Roman Emperor in the West, and the Ottoman sultan (whom the Russians called tsar as well).

The reign of Ivan IV, which lasted until his death in 1584, is one of the most controversial epochs in Russian history. Virtually every event and detail is the object of complex disputes, unfortunately many of them inspired more by putative analogies to the Stalin era than by the desire to comprehend the sixteenth century.

In some respects, the reign of Ivan was highly successful, both for himself and for Russia. In 1552–56 his armies conquered first the Khanate of Kazan' and then that of Astrakhan' at the mouth of the Volga. The whole river and its basin were now Russian territory, the first major wedge into the western extension of the Eurasian steppe. Russia acquired huge, fertile territories that later generations would turn into the heartlands of Russian agriculture. The Russians built their first fort on the Terek River in 1567, looking into Circassia, Chechnya, and other districts of the northern Caucasus mountains.

In the 1550s Ivan began to build up a more effective state apparatus. The administration he inherited was simply too small and primitive to support the growing size and population of Russia. He established new central offices (*prikazy*) to administer, judge, and tax the country. The foreign policy functions of the treasury were split off to form the Ambassadorial Office, a center not only for the conduct of foreign policy but also for the beginnings of greater cultural contact with Europe and Asia. He abolished the old system of supporting local administration by "feeding," putting the collection of taxes into the hands of local rural and urban communities and ordering the election of local gentry as judges and policemen. Gradually the need for greater control led him to begin to appoint local governors (*voevody*) to exercise the police and judicial functions and supervise the collection of taxes. These men were taken from the lesser-ranked landholders and paid a salary by the treasury, and often changed every year. The great border fortresses—Novgorod, Smolensk, Astrakhan'—remained the preserve of the boyars. To improve the army, Ivan began to restrict the operation of the precedence system during military campaigns and formed several regiments of foot soldiers carrying the new matchlock muskets, the *strel'tsy*. Ivan also tried to restrict the financial autonomy of the church while encouraging its spiritual hegemony over the country.

Most of these changes came in the early years of his reign, 1547–60. In 1558 Ivan moved in a new direction that was the beginning of a period of violence and confusion. Ivan was not content with the vast acquisitions in the Volga; he also wanted access to the Baltic Sea. Strictly speaking, he already had it, since Novgorod and later Russia had possessed the mouth of the Neva River since time immemorial, the site where St. Petersburg now stands. However, the site was swampy and unsuited for building with sixteenth-century technology, so most of Russia's trade with the West went through what is today Estonia and Latvia, then three districts, Estonia, Livonia, and Kurland, usually known today as Livonia for short. Livonia in 1558 was still the property of the Teutonic Order, a crusading order of knights founded in the thirteenth century to reconquer Jerusalem from the Muslims. Since that attempt had proved unsuccessful, the Teutonic knights turned their attention to the eastern shores of the Baltic, where the Prussians, Lithuanians, Latvians, and Estonians remained poly-theistic in religion. The absence of Christianity gave the knights the justification they needed and papal approval to conquer the territory. The Prussians were exterminated, leaving only their name to the German state that arose on their land. Lithuania, then beginning its rise to power, was able to fend off the Teutonic knights at the cost of endless fighting. Latvia and Estonia were conquered by the knights, who then planted German cities and a German landholding class in the territory. This German ruling elite still dominated Livonia's state and society in the 1550s, but the spread of the Reformation undermined its political structure, based as it was on a Catholic order of knight-monks. The Ger-man rulers began to look to Poland, Sweden, and even Russia to provide an anchor for the territory.

Ivan did not want to wait for events, and in 1558 his armies invaded Livonia, taking Narva and Dorpat in the first year. Thus he began a war that lasted almost a quarter of a century, in which Russia received absolutely nothing and Livonia was eventually divided between Poland and Sweden. It seems that some of the Russian boyars may have opposed the war altogether, and it is certainly true that the ongoing effort drained Russian resources and seriously exacerbated internal conflicts.

Whatever the origins of these conflicts, Ivan's relations with much of the boyar aristocracy deteriorated after 1558. In December 1564, Tsar Ivan suddenly abandoned the Kremlin and Moscow and went off to the nearby town of Alexandrovo, taking his family and the treasury with him. He sent a message to the metropolitan announcing that the boyars were traitors and he would no longer rule with them. The response was a petition by the church, the people of Moscow, and the boyars begging him to return. Ivan agreed, but when he returned, he divided the country into two administrative districts, one called the Zemshchina, ruled by the old Boyar Duma, and the other the Oprichnina, which he ruled with a new administration composed of his supporters. The new structure gave him the basis he needed to attack many of his enemies. Dozens of boyars were executed or exiled, and many hundreds of their relatives and clients followed them. Ivan's reach went far beyond the boyar elite, and eventually the toll was several thousand. The policy of repression continued only a few years, and by 1572 the violence was over. The boyar families who had suffered during the period of the Oprichnina remained out of the Duma and out of power until Ivan's death in 1584.

The whole episode remains obscure and controversial. Was it an attempt at greater power for the tsar? Was it an attack on the boyar aristocracy? Was it the result of Ivan's decision to take sides in boyar rivalries? Was it the result of personal paranoia? Insofar as it was an attack on the boyar aristocracy, the policy was clearly a failure, for after his death the clans whom he had exiled returned to the Duma. The boyar elite included the same families as before. One result, however, was that the rivalries among the elite families in the Duma reached a pitch unseen since the regency of 1533–47. The great families, Shuiskii, Obolenskii, Romanov, Mstislavskii, and others, took advantage of the weakness of Tsar Fyodor Ivanovich (1584–98) to attack one another with exile and execution. The ultimate outcome of the rivalries among the boyars was the election of Boris Godunov as tsar in 1598 when the Riurikovich dynasty came to end.

Boris did not come from a great boyar family. He had risen from the middle ranks of the landholding class through the Oprichnina and then through his sister's marriage to Tsar Fyodor. By the end of his brother-in-law's reign he had become the power behind the throne, so it is no surprise that the Assembly of the Land, that is, the boyars, the clergy, and representatives of the lesser landholders and the towns, were easily persuaded to elect him the tsar. The position was open because Tsar Fyodor had no children, and the other son of Ivan IV, Tsarevich Dmitrii, died in a mysterious accident in 1591. The story was that Dmitrii fell on a toy sword while playing, but many suspected that Boris had him murdered. Dmitrii's mysterious death gave the opportunity for one Grishka Otrep'ev, a runaway monk, to go to Poland and proclaim himself to be the rightful heir by pretending that he was Tsarevich Dmitrii miraculously preserved from death.

The period of upheaval and anarchy that followed, known as the Time of Troubles, was naturally the product of much more than the personal ambitions of the False Dmitrii, as Otrep'ev came to be known. The last years of the sixteenth century saw the beginnings of serfdom in Russia. The previously free Russian peasantry began to fall under the power of the landholding class, as the peasantry's right to move freely from estate to estate was more and more restricted by law. Changing custom did the rest, and the peasant tenant had to perform onerous labor services (*barshchina*) or pay rent (*obrok*) for the use of the land. Only in the north, the Urals, Siberia, and the southern border did the peasants remain free of the landholder's power. On the southern border the tsar needed men to defend the settlements against the Tatar raiders, and these were the Cossacks. Free men and skilled fighters on horseback, the Cossacks of the southern borders took in more and more peasants fleeing south to escape the growing burdens of serfdom. Thus when the False Dmitrii crossed from Polish territory into southern Russia in August 1604, he found the fuel ready for a social and political conflagration.

Perhaps Dmitrii's efforts would have sparked only a short-lived Cossack and peasant revolt like so many others were it not for the dissension among the boyar elite. When Boris Godunov suddenly died in April 1605, his generals did not swear allegiance to his son and fight the False Dmitrii; instead all three of them, P. S. Basmanov and the Princes I. V. and V. V. Golitsyn, joined the pretender. Thus the False Dmitrii went on to take Moscow and to be crowned the new tsar. The exiled enemies of Boris among the boyars, Prince Bogdan Bel'skii and the Romanov clan, returned from exile to take up positions at the pretender's court.

The pretender lasted less than a year. His Polish entourage offended the Russian people and the Russian elite, who had suffered under Boris and had no intention of sharing power with foreign nobles. In May 1606, the boyars and the mob in Moscow overthrew the False Dmitrii and killed him as well as many of his Polish followers. Prince Vasilii Shuiskii, another old opponent of Boris Godunov among the boyars, was elected tsar. His election did not bring peace. Social revolts continued in southern Russia, and a new False Dmitrii appeared in 1608, again with Polish and Cossack support. His army established a camp just outside Moscow at the village of Tushino, and many prominent boyars came to support him or at least to give the impression that they would. Most prominent was Filaret Romanov, head of the Romanov clan. Filaret was the monastic name of the boyar Fyodor Nikitich Romanov, exiled in 1600 by Boris Godunov and forced to become a monk. The first False Dmitrii appointed him metropolitan of Rostov, and the second proclaimed him patriarch. Thus two of the greatest boyar clans, the Princes Shuiskii and the Romanovs, were at odds.

Their rivalry had its most disastrous effects on the invasion of Russia by King Sigismund of Poland, which began late in 1609.

As Sigismund besieged Smolensk, many of the Tushino boyars, including the Romanovs, decided to make a deal with him to accept his son Wladyslaw as tsar on condition that he would convert to Orthodoxy. Then in summer 1610, the boyars in Moscow overthrew Shuiskii, leaving the throne vacant. The boyars called the Assembly of the Land, which offered the throne to Wladyslaw under pressure from the Polish army. The Poles entered Moscow. As with the first False Dmitrii, Polish ambitions proved their undoing. Wladyslaw's father King Sigismund wanted to rule Russia himself and add it to the Catholic fold, two measures that were guaranteed to bring about a revolt. That is exactly what happened: Provincial nobles and townspeople, spurred on by the church, came together to form an army under Prince Dmitrii Pozharskii that defeated the Poles and retook Moscow at the end of 1612. The boyars followed in their wake, thus making it possible to hold on to their traditional position in the state. On February 7, 1613, the Assembly of the Land chose a new tsar, Michael Romanov, the sixteen-year-old son of Filaret Romanov. Another five years of fighting was needed to restore order and make peace with Poland and Sweden, but after Michael's election the end was in sight.

THE SEVENTEENTH CENTURY

Russia at the close of the Troubles was a wreck. Smolensk and the Baltic coast had been lost to Poland and Sweden. Large areas were devastated, taking a whole generation to recover the population and restore agriculture. What Russia did have was a strong government again, especially after Filaret returned from Polish captivity in 1619. Soon elected patriarch of the Orthodox Church in Russia, he exercised overwhelming influence on his son until his death in 1633. Part of the strength of Michael's government was also the radical reduction in tension at court. Seemingly the boyars learned from the Time of Troubles, and though the rivalries and jockeying for position continued, they never attained the ferocity of the sixteenth century. In the whole period from 1613 to 1676, only two members of the Duma were executed (both over the Smolensk War of 1632–34) and a dozen exiled, almost all for brief periods and most of them during the patriarchate of Filaret.

Relative calm at court did not imply peace in the country at large. The reign of Michael's son Aleksei (1645–76) was fraught with conflict. In 1648–50 attempts to reform the tax system and other issues led to a series of riots in Moscow, Novgorod, Pskov, and other towns. Patriarch Nikon's reform of the liturgy of the church beginning in 1653 led in the ensuing years to a profound schism in the Orthodox Church of Russia, which has lasted to the present day. In 1662 adulteration of the currency produced another major upheaval in Moscow (the "Copper Revolt"). Finally, in 1670–71 the Don Cossack Stenka Razin led thousands of Cossacks and peasants in the first of Russia's great rural uprisings, a revolt that covered almost the whole of the Volga and involved Tatars, Mordovians, and other native peoples besides the Russian peasants and Cossacks. Aleksei had to send the army to crush it.

Russia was hardly at peace abroad. In 1648 the Hetman, the elected commander, of the Ukrainian Cossacks, Bohdan Khmel'nyts'kyi, began a massive revolt in the name of Cossack rights and Orthodox religion against Polish rule in Ukraine. Initially Aleksei was mainly interested in preserving peace with Poland but in 1653 he acceded to repeated Ukrainian entreaties to take them "under his high hand." The treaty with the Ukrainian Cossacks made them the tsar's subjects with an autonomous government headed by the Cossack Hetman. Russia declared war on Poland, and fighting continued until 1667 with a victorious conclusion for Russia. Tsar Aleksei recaptured Smolensk and confirmed the annexation of the Ukraine east of the Dnieper and the city of Kiev. As we shall see, this was an event full of major cultural implications.

During most of his reign Aleksei made no attempt to alter the balance of power among the great boyar families. At the time of the Moscow revolt of 1648, the most powerful boyar was Boris Morozov, the descendant of boyars back to the fourteenth century.[2] He had been Tsar Aleksei's tutor, and after 1645 seems to have been behind the new taxation policies that earned him the hatred of the mob. His allies who perished in the revolt were lesser men, perhaps more his clients than his allies. His opponents in the elite were Prince Ia. K. Cherkasskii and N. I. Romanov, both boyars and cousins of Tsar Aleksei. The events divided the Romanov clan, pitting the eldest Romanov against his cousin the tsar. After the return of Morozov to court he recovered some influence, but the period 1649–71 saw a variety of families with influence. The Miloslavskii relatives of Tsar Aleksei's first wife, Maria, naturally had high position and importance, but Aleksei showed great favor to the Princes Romodanovskii, to Bogdan Khitrovo (a boyar of middle-rank origins who headed the palace offices), and to his son's tutor, the *okol'nichii* F. M. Rtishchev. He gave important military commands and offices to boyars who seemed to have had no personal ties to the tsar, such as the Sheremetevs and the Princes Odoevskii and Dolgorukii. While Nikon held the patriarchate (1652–58), he exerted wide influence in and outside of the church. During these years the political groupings were small, and we know too little of the politics of the time to confidently assert that personal ties or policy issues bound together the various groups.

After the 1667 treaty with Poland, however, the tsar began to change his policy. For the final treaty negotiations Aleksei sent A. L. Ordin-Nashchokin, a landholder and soldier of middle rank whom the tsar singled out for his ability and knowledge of the West and Poland. In doing so Aleksei bypassed the boyars, Princes Odoevskii and Dolgorukii, who had headed earlier Russian delegations to the discussions. He soon appointed Ordin-Nashchokin head of the Ambassadorial Office that coordinated

Russia's foreign policy. The new favorite's charge was to secure peace with Poland and guard against the revived power of the Ottoman Turks, now Russia's neighbor because of Ottoman suzerainty over the Tatar Khanate of Crimea. Russian control of the Ukraine meant that Russia was now directly confronting Crimea and the Turks. When Ordin-Nashchokin proved unsuccessful at his task, Aleksei replaced him with Artamon Sergeevich Matveev. This appointment was the harbinger of a new and unsettling policy.

Tsar Aleksei not only placed Matveev at the head of Russia's foreign policy, but allowed him to appoint his clients, such as the clerk G. L. Dokhturov, to run most of the other major offices. Though Matveev had to bring his policies for discussion to the Boyar Duma, he was sure of getting his way if the tsar supported him, and the tsar usually did. Matveev's power was further ensured by the marriage of the widowed tsar to Natalia Naryshkina, the daughter of Kirill Naryshkin, a fellow officer of the *strel'tsy*. Naryshkin had served under Matveev before he received his own regiment, and after the marriage the Naryshkins began to enter the Duma. Matveev was able to secure the marriage in spite of the opposition of Tsar Aleksei's elder sister, Tsarevna Irina. Tsar Aleksei came to rely on Matveev, the "kinglet" in the words of Danish Ambassador Mogens Gjøe, though in origin Matveev was simply a provincial nobleman and a commander of one of the privileged Moscow *strel'tsy* regiments. The Naryshkins were exactly the same sort of people. Neither family came from the boyar elite, and only the tsar's favor kept Matveev in high position. When Tsar Aleksei suddenly died in January 1676, Matveev quickly fell from power, an event with far-reaching consequences.

Despite Tsar Aleksei's attempt in his last years to circumvent the boyar elite, it remained the most powerful group in Russia, holders of the key positions in government as well as the richest component in society. Let us look at the structure of that power and wealth.

The Boyar Duma itself gradually increased in number in the years from 1613 to the end of the century. In 1613–14 there were about twenty men with the rank of boyar and eight with the rank of *okol'nichii*. These numbers increased only marginally in Michael's time, to about twenty-five and ten respectively. In the reign of Tsar Aleksei, however, the number of *okol'nichie* grew to about twenty-five. The lesser ranks also increased in number, the duma gentlemen (*dumnye dvoriane*) to about fifteen by the end of the 1660s, and the Duma secretaries from one or two in Michael's time to five or six. As the number of boyars remained approximately constant, by the end of Aleksei's reign the holders of boyar rank were considerably outnumbered by the other members of the Duma. Only after 1676 did the number of boyars expand to around fifty, a third of the Duma by the 1690s. The particularly rapid increase in numbers after 1676 probably reflected the attempt by weak rulers to reward potential supporters, but the overall increase in the size of the elite reflected larger social changes. From about the 1640s on, recent research on boyar landholding and demography suggests a threefold increase in numbers and in wealth among the landholding class.

The increased wealth of the landholding class after the 1640s made the boyars into great magnates of enormous wealth. Some of the great clans owned fifty or sixty thousand peasants and gigantic tracts of land, which these peasants worked. The boyars tended to own the best of Russia's lands, the rich lands on the northern edge of the steppe. They also held many of the trading and artisanal villages of central Russia, for much of Russia's trade and crafts by 1700 took place not in towns but in villages. The boyar Morozov owned several such villages near Nizhnii Novgorod, whose population, enserfed peasants in legal status, journeyed every year to the northern port of Archangel to trade with the English and Dutch ships that were the mainstay of Russia's foreign trade. All these far-flung holdings the boyars supervised by correspondence with bailiffs, some of them their own serfs, scattered throughout their estates. The boyars could maintain enormous retinues of servants, sometimes several hundred in their Moscow houses alone, and the ostentatious display of jewelry, furs, imported textiles, decorated and jewel-encrusted sabers and other weapons from Iran and the Ottoman Empire, and huge stables and hunting preserves became the hallmark of the boyar's household and private life. Boyars paid for elaborate church buildings in Moscow and on their country estates, and contributed large sums of money, icons, and rich vestments to the great monasteries, especially those where their families were buried.

The political and administrative role of the boyars was undiminished until the rise of Artamon Matveev. Until 1671 most of the main chancelleries, the *prikazy*, were under the leadership of the boyars. Some boyars, like Aleksei's father-in-law Il'ia Miloslavskii, held several offices at once in the 1650s. After Matveev's rise the boyars lost most of the chancelleries, but they continued to hold down the major provincial governorships, in Novgorod, Pskov, Kazan', and Astrakhan'. After the capture of Smolensk and Kiev, these positions also went to men from the great clans. The major military commands in the army continued to go to the great boyars as well, Sheremetev and Princes Odoevskii and Dolgorukii. Most important diplomatic missions were still headed by great boyars. In all these cases the boyar usually had a second-in-command, normally a younger man from a lesser family (who often did most of the work), but the boyar remained at the head. Finally, the boyars still served the tsar in various court positions. The Russian court grew much larger and more elaborate in the second half of the seventeenth century, and needed a larger and larger staff to conduct ceremonies and the daily life of the court. Aleksei began the practice of appointing the sons of the great boyars (and some young men of lesser rank) to the rank of chamber *stol'nik*. In the sixteenth century *stol'niki* (*stol* = table) had literally attended the tsar's table, supervising the actual servants.

Originally the rank was awarded as the highest rank below the Duma ranks, and only a few dozen men received it. After about 1650, the number of *stol'niki* increased to nearly two thousand, the main upper middle rank in the landholding class, an indication of status rather than any specific position. Chamber *stol'niki*, by contrast, were few in number (eighteen in 1664, forty-four in 1682), and had the privilege of serving the tsar's person directly. The tsaritsa and other close relatives of the tsar also had chamber *stol'niki* of their own, which put the sons of the elite in direct contact with the ruling dynasty from their youth onward.

The most important of the political activities were in the Duma. We know very little about the actual functioning of the Boyar Duma, for its proceedings were not written down and in theory were secret. Nevertheless it is clear from the reports of foreign diplomats that the major issues of foreign policy were discussed there, even when the tsar had already determined his own views. It seems that there was a certain division of labor in legislation, with military matters and civil appointments decided by the tsar alone and other issues, such as land questions and taxation, decided by the tsar in consultation with the Boyar Duma. Whatever the formal role of the Boyar Duma, the informal power of the boyars was great, especially of those with the tsar's favor. Until the rise of Matveev, however, Tsar Aleksei never allowed any one of the great boyars to overbalance the others, and usually maintained several powerful men at his court at any one time.

The informal politics of the court in the seventeenth century is crucial to the understanding of the Russian state, but unfortunately they are known only imperfectly. Some historians have argued that the family alliances were the most important organizing principle of boyar politics.[3] The formal system of precedence as well as pride in ancestry and clan certainly encouraged this tendency, and frequently we see brothers or fathers and sons in the same factional grouping at court. At the same time, families could be politically divided, as was common during the Time of Troubles. Again in the 1680s the Princes Golitsyn were on opposite sides of the major political division of the time. One family tie that was critical was marriage into the ruling Romanov dynasty. After the time of Vasilii III, Russian rulers did not seek foreign princesses for their wives, and chose them from among the native landholding class. After the first marriage of Ivan IV to Anastasia Romanova, the tsar also did not choose brides from among the elite, preferring women of lesser rank. Apparently the purpose was to avoid the political complications that might ensue from a very aristocratic marriage, and the result was that a number of provincial landholders suddenly were promoted to the highest ranks in the land. The Princes Dolgorukii recovered their earlier status in the 1620s through such a marriage, and soon claimed to be an "ancient family," only a partial truth. The Streshnev, Miloslavskii, and Naryshkin clans owed their high rank entirely to such a marriage. Usually these relatives of the tsar would support him in the disagreements that arose, but not always. The Romanov clan was no more united than the great boyar clans.

It was Tsar Aleksei's decision to put Artamon Matveev in a position of unique power and influence that unbalanced the system in 1671–76. The Russian political system as it existed after 1613 had several distinctive features. Serious consultation with the population was minimal, occurring only when the throne was vacant as in 1598 and 1613. In normal times, it was the tsar and boyars who administered and ruled Russia. Their relationship was a complex one, composed of the theoretically unlimited power of the tsar and the customary predominance of the great families, primarily the old boyar clans and some new promotions. Custom and the precedence system maintained the great clans in positions of power and influence from the fourteenth century onward. Among the great clans, it was not princely titles but their traditional role in the Russian state that determined their formal and informal position. The great clans were jealous of their prerogatives and proud of their ancestry and in many respects tried to keep the clan as a whole, not just a few individual members of it, at the pinnacle of the state. Nevertheless, the clans were not necessarily united on all issues. Matters of policy or just jockeying for position or favor sometimes divided them internally.

In all this the tsar did not play a passive role. His position as tsar gave him tremendous power. He alone made appointments to all civil and military positions, even if he had to contend with the precedence system and the traditional leadership role of the aristocracy. He was the source of law, even if foreign policy and most domestic matters were settled with the consultation of the Boyar Duma. His informal power was great as well. The tsar's relatives occupied a unique place in the hierarchy. Every new marriage of the monarch brought a new family to instant wealth and high position, providing him with immediate allies. Reliance on this or that faction of the court aristocracy gave him strength as well, just as he gave strength to the factions he favored. Finally the tsar had his favorites. This practice could be explosive, as in 1648 with Morozov, but most of the time Tsars Michael and Aleksei managed to rely on some of the great men without offending the others. The exception to this rule was the ascendancy of Matveev in the court and the government, which came to a sudden end with the death of the tsar. In giving such power to Matveev, Aleksei set off a chain of events with far-reaching consequences.

NOTES

1. His battle with the Teutonic knights on Lake Peipus (1242) would be the subject of a famous film, *Alexander Nevsky*, by Sergei Eisenstein (1939).

2. Morozov's ancestors had been in the Boyar Duma without serious interruption since 1476, surviving both Ivan the Terrible and the Time of Troubles.

3. See the works of Nancy Kollmann and John LeDonne listed in "Further Reading" below.

FURTHER READING

Alef, Gustave. "The Origins of Muscovite Autocracy: The Age of Ivan III," *Forschungen zur Geschichte Osteuropas* 39 (1986).

Crummey, Robert O. *Aristocrats and Servitors: The Boyar Elite of Russia 1613–1689*. Princeton, NJ: Princeton University Press, 1983.

——. *The Formation of Muscovy 1304–1613*. London: Longman's, 1987.

Fennell, John. *A History of the Russian Church to 1448*. London: Longman's, 1995.

Kleimola, Ann M. "The Changing Face of the Muscovite Autocracy. The Sixteenth Century: Sources of Weakness," *Jahrbücher für Geschichte Osteuropas* 25 (1977): 481–93.

Kollmann, Nancy Shields. *Kinship and Politics: The Making of the Muscovite Political System 1345–1547*. Stanford, CA: Stanford University Press, 1987.

LeDonne, John P. "Ruling Families in the Russian Political Order 1689–1825," *Cahiers du Monde russe et sovietique* XXVIII, nos. 3–4 (1987): 233–322.

Martin, Janet. *Medieval Russia 980–1584*. Cambridge, UK: Cambridge University Press, 1995.

Platonov, S. F. *The Time of Troubles*. Trans. John T. Alexander. Lawrence: University Press of Kansas Press, 1970.

Skrynnikov, R. G. *Boris Godunov*. Ed. and trans. Hugh F. Graham, Gulf Breeze, FL: Academic International Press, 1982.

——. *Ivan the Terrible*. Ed. and trans. Hugh F. Graham, Gulf Breeze, FL: Academic International Press, 1981.

Chapter Two

Tradition and Westernization

The Westernization of Russian culture was the most permanent effect of Peter's reign, and it outlasted almost all of his other achievements. To understand the process, we need to know what we mean by Westernization. At the most basic level, it simply means the adoption of Western, that is to say European, cultural norms and practice in addition to or in place of those traditional to Russia. Neither Peter nor his subjects adopted the whole of European culture: They chose some aspects and not others, and the degree of Europeanization varied greatly in society. The locus of this Europeanization was in the Russian court elite and to a lesser extent in the church, with the result that Europeanization was at first an elite phenomenon. Within that elite the most powerful force for Westernization after 1689 was the tsar himself. It was Peter's will that enormously speeded the process and brought Russia into Europe.

European culture in 1700 was not a uniform, undifferentiated essence, as it is often described in accounts of Peter's reign. Indeed no historian of Europe would put in one camp the enormous variety of European culture, divided by local traditions, social and regional distinctions, national states, religion, and varying degrees of involvement in new trends. European culture had been changing rapidly since the end of the Middle Ages and continued to evolve as the Russians came to learn of it. They jumped into a moving river.

What Peter and his contemporaries found in Europe was the last phase of what we call the age of the Baroque. Originally a term in art history, Baroque refers to the artistic style cultivated in the churches and palaces of seventeenth-century Europe. Baroque art built on the Renaissance with its classical models but transformed it into a more florid, more monumental, mode of expression particularly adapted to glorify God and powerful monarchs. Not all of European art from the time fits this model. It flourished in Italy, Spain, and Central Europe, but much of the north, particularly the Netherlands, went in other directions. Seventeenth-century European culture was not confined to Baroque art. This was the age of the scientific revolution, the construction of a mathematical explanation of the universe that broke with Aristotelian teleology. Galileo, Johannes Kepler, Isaac Newton, and Gottfried Leibniz constructed a new picture of the solar system and in the process evolved a new physics and a new mathematics that opened up vast arenas to human understanding. In philosophy it was the period of rationalism, where René Descartes, Thomas Hobbes, Benedict Spinoza, and Leibniz tried to work out the principles of human knowledge, ethics, and the state from rational deduction alone, ignoring both Aristotle and revealed religion.

At the same time many of the new ideas only penetrated slowly into society. Education for most people, even of the elite, remained quite conservative in Baroque Europe, based on the Renaissance tradition of intense study of Latin and Greek and Renaissance rhetoric. After these subjects, the student went on to the study of Aristotle, who still formed the basis of all knowledge in schools throughout Europe. The Russians encountered this complicated cultural world with its many layers and conflicts, and had to choose what they would take. Not surprisingly, the Russians of Peter's time mostly took in the average school culture of the elite, not Newton and Descartes. It was the generation after Peter that went on to absorb these newer ideas.

The interest in European culture came from the court, that is from the tsar himself and his family and from the court elite, the boyars. The church played a role here as well, in spite of the resistance of much of the provincial clergy to the new trends. Thus what Russia got from the West was European culture as it was practiced at European courts and among the aristocracy, not the culture of the towns or of institutions that depended on new economic forces and social forms emerging since the fifteenth century. Printing is a good example, for in Europe it flourished in the cities and freer states like England and Holland that were also increasingly urban in structure, not in France, where the censorship was too strict.

In Russia printing had to be fostered by the tsar, and long after Peter's time, when independent printers came into existence, their largest problem was not censorship but the lack of a market. Education similarly reflected Russian conditions. Private tutors to aristocratic families took the place of organized schools, which were few in number and small in size well into the eighteenth century. Thus for some Russian noblemen Europeanization was quite superficial, while others found themselves more fluent in French than in their native language. The elite character of the process also implied that it did not reach down very far, scarcely into the urban population and not at all into the peasantry.

In Peter's time the influence of European culture came to Russia by different paths. We know most about Peter's efforts, his orders to young noblemen to study abroad, his pensions for young artists, his establishment of schools and printing, his encouragement of translations of secular learning into Russian, and his building of St. Petersburg, a wholly new cultural model for Russia. Another important channel of influence was the Europeans whom Peter brought to Russia to work and teach. These men were many and varied, such as his Scottish personal physician

Robert Erskine; Baron Heinrich Huyssen, his official publicist; Jean-Baptiste Leblond, the architect and garden designer; and the architects Domenico Trezzini, Giovanni Maria Fontana, Andreas Schlüter, and others. We know much less about the effect of all this on the Russians, and the paths of cultural influence beyond those officially sponsored and financed.

Peter himself played the central role in the process of Europeanization, but paradoxically one in which his personal tastes were not necessarily the most influential. The autocratic Peter was obsessed with the Dutch Republic, mainly its mariners, shipbuilders, and engineers. Dutch was the only foreign language Peter knew well, and later when he attempted to learn and speak German the mixture that ensued tried the comprehension and good humor of many a foreign guest. He was fascinated with Dutch painting and architecture, with mathematics, navigation, and technology, but few of these interests attracted followers. Most Russians preferred the average culture of the European nobleman, with its mixture of Latin and modern languages, some knowledge of the classics, and a greater acquaintance with modern history and political affairs. They preferred Italian architecture and painting to the Dutch, and the usual foreign language of Russians in Peter's time was German. The Europeanization of Russian culture was not just the tsar imposing his tastes on the country. The Russian aristocracy chose what appealed to them from the panoply of European culture, and their choices were frequently quite different from Peter's.

Finally, we need to remember that the notion of "Europeanization" is a modern one, implying as it does the substitution of one national tradition for another. Europeans and Russians of 1700 did not think that "Europe" had a better culture than Russia; they thought that Russia lacked learning and the arts (as they put it), whereas Europe did not, for it had passed through the revival of learning and the arts in the Renaissance. They thought that Europe had something universal to offer, knowledge and learning, not merely a national tradition. Russia lacked that learning, and the acquisition of it was merely a question of will, resources, and time. Russia would enter the world of light and knowledge, not "Europe."

RUSSIAN TRADITION

Before the end of the seventeenth century the mental world of the boyar elite, the tsar, his court, and Russia as a whole was very different from that of Western Europe for it was almost entirely religious. Western Europe, even in the Middle Ages, and Byzantium both had cultures with complex secular elements. Both societies produced poetry and prose with secular themes, had extensive histories that described much more than simply divine intervention in human affairs, and had an extensive scientific and legal literature. None of this existed in Russia before the end of the seventeenth century.

The reasons for this overwhelming predominance of religion go deep into Russian history. When Kiev Rus' accepted Christianity from the Byzantines in 988, the new church used a Slavonic liturgy and literary language. The Slavonic liturgy may have brought Christian faith more readily to the people of Rus', but it also meant that they did not learn Greek. Therefore the people of Kiev Rus' had no access to the wealth of ancient Greek literature and learning that was so carefully cultivated in the Byzantine court and society. The people of medieval Russia who could read had only the works of the Greek fathers, the lives of the saints, and the literature of monastic spirituality that had been translated into Slavonic. The Byzantines read and commented on the works of Plato, for example, but the Russians knew nothing of Plato or his commentators.

Perhaps medieval Russia before 1500 was just too small and peripheral a society to support much of a secular culture of its own, or presumed secular elements like heroic tales and songs remained an oral literature now lost to us. In either case, the only substantial body of Russian literature of the period that is not devotional is the medieval Russian chronicles, the laconic accounts of battles and the foundation of churches that make up medieval Russian history. During the fifteenth century, however, changes came, particularly a great increase in original Russian works of piety. Relying at first on monks from Serbia and Bulgaria, Russia began to produce lives of the major Russian saints and other religious texts. The Greek monastic writer Maksim the Greek (Michael Trivolis, c. 1470–1555) widened Russian horizons to include some of the linguistic accomplishments of Renaissance Italy, though his attitude toward the Renaissance as a whole was unfriendly. Maksim had worked in Venice and Florence, copying classical Greek manuscripts. He lived in the center of Renaissance culture, but was ultimately more impressed by the religious reformer Girolamo Savonarola's call for a return to true piety. In his own works, Greek and Russian, Maksim rejected the Renaissance as a semipagan distraction from Christian faith. In his lifetime Maksim was imprisoned twice by his enemies in the Russian Church and had few followers. His works survived, however, and were widely read through the seventeenth century, when they had an important impact on the Old Believers. Not surprisingly, what impact Maksim did have on the laity in his lifetime was confined to the court elite.[1]

The religion that formed the basis of Russian culture was Eastern Orthodoxy. Westerners often think of Orthodoxy as a sort of Slavic or Greek Catholicism, but that assumption is misleading. Orthodoxy is simply the traditional Christian church of the East, which survived in those areas after the disagreements of the Papacy and the Patriarchs of Constantinople led to a split that occurred in the eleventh and twelfth centuries. The differences in teaching about the basic elements of faith were never profound, especially compared with the split in the West during the Reformation. The disagreements between Orthodoxy and Catholicism revolved around the way that the doctrine of the Trinity was presented in the Creed, and other very refined points, as well as matters of liturgical practice.

More significant were the differences in church customs and government. Orthodox priests remained married as they had been before the division of the churches, while the bishops and patriarchs were selected from the ranks of the monks who were celibate. The Orthodox Church is a conciliar church: that is, the nominal heads of the church, the Patriarchs of Constantinople or of Moscow, do not have either the administrative power or the power of defining doctrine that the Pope possesses. A council of the church is required to decide such matters in the East. In the West from the eleventh century onward the Papacy was often in conflict with the secular authorities, claiming both independent powers and even the right to depose kings. In the East the theory was that the Byzantine emperor and the patriarch should work in harmony. In both cases, the reality was often different: The medieval monarchs of Europe seriously eroded papal power by the end of the Middle Ages, and in the East the emperor was often much stronger than the patriarch. The theoretical differences, however, were significant in preserving different ideals of church government. Finally, the Orthodox Church in Byzantium and even more in Russia saw no reason to cultivate and incorporate secular culture into its own teaching. In the West, Saint Thomas Aquinas and other philosophers used Aristotle's teachings to build a monumental structure of Catholic theology. In the East, most theologians thought such attempts were essentially useless and ignored Aristotle or other philosophers in their writings.[2] All of these differences made for rather different practices and religious life, though the Catholic and Orthodox churches have remained very close in their formal dogmatic teachings.

The other characteristic feature of Orthodoxy, especially in Russia, was the enormous spiritual authority of the monasteries. In the medieval West, monasteries were crucially important to spiritual life, but the church hierarchy centered on the bishops. The Catholic cathedral churches with their bishops were also major centers of cult and devotion. Orthodox bishops in Russia were rather shadowy figures both on the administrative and spiritual level, working in the background of the great spiritual drama of monasticism. Starting in the fourteenth century, Russian monasticism went through a period of intense revival, producing such major figures as Saint Sergii of Radonezh, Saint Kirill of Belozero, and Saints Zosima and Savvatii, all of whom founded major monasteries. Pafnutii of Borovsk, Joseph of Volokolamsk, and Nil Sorskii all provided examples of monastic piety and composed many writings to explain to others how to follow them, as well as arguments over the correct path to follow. One such argument was that over the proper role of monastic landholding, where Vassian Patrikeev, born a prince in a boyar family, defended restrictions on landholding. After the middle of the sixteenth century, the monks seem to have produced fewer saints and fewer devotional tracts, but the monasteries remained major centers of piety for clergy and laity alike.

The monasteries were a particularly large part of the life of the tsars and the boyars. The tsars were major patrons of the monasteries, giving them extensive lands, illuminated manuscripts, jeweled reliquaries and silver communion cups, many icons from the tsar's palace workshop, and sometimes just cash. Some of the donations were to support prayers for dead relatives, or as in the case of Ivan the Terrible, prayers for the souls of his victims during the Oprichnina. Other donations were just gifts to help the monastery. Every year, from at least the fifteenth century, the Moscow princes and their successors the tsars went on several pilgrimages to pray at the major monasteries. The most common and most important was the journey to the monastery of Saint Sergii of Radonezh near Moscow for his feast day (September 25), but if the tsar was in good health, he went to many others, even as far as the great northern monastery of Saint Kirill at Belozero. The tsars sometimes acquired a particular interest in one or another of the monasteries, such as that of Tsar Aleksei for the Saint Savva Storozhevskii monastery, also near Moscow.

The boyars as well had particular monasteries that they favored. Boyars rarely became monks themselves (most monks came from the provincial landholding class), but they patronized the monasteries. They gave the same sorts of gifts as the tsars, and requested the same prayers for the dead. Particular boyar clans buried their dead in particular monasteries, especially those in and around Moscow. The Princes Golitsyn favored the Trinity–Saint Sergii Monastery and later the Epiphany Monastery in Moscow. The Princes Dolgorukii in the seventeenth century preferred the Epiphany Monastery as well, and the Romanovs the New Monastery of the Savior just outside Moscow. The Naryshkins, the family of Peter's mother, chose the Vysoko-Petrovskii Monastery near the outer wall of Moscow, and almost totally rebuilt it in the 1690s. The family of Peter's wife, the Lopukhins, took over patronage of the ancient Andronikov Monastery just outside Moscow to the south about the same time. In the seventeenth century the boyars became an important source of patronage for church building. Boyars built private chapels in their Moscow houses, a practice the church disapproved of but could not stop. In their estates they paid for stone churches to replace the older wooden ones, a sign of the new prosperity of the last half of the seventeenth century. The boyars rivaled one another in the richness of the churches they built in and around Moscow, a practice that would have important artistic and cultural consequences.

CHURCH REFORM AND WESTERNIZATION

This was the traditional world of Russian culture. In the seventeenth century, beginning soon after the end of the Time of Troubles, Russian culture began to change. The reasons for the

changes are probably to be found in the growing complexity of
Russian state and society, as its population and wealth increased
and the tsars tried to cope with more complex tasks in domestic
and foreign policy. The impulse for change came from within
Russia, and particularly from inside the church. These new currents in the Orthodox Church originally had nothing to do with
Westernization, but coming to the fore as they did in the middle
of the seventeenth century, they strengthened the impulse toward
Westernization. Paradoxically, the Orthodox Church, which was
the basis of Russia's uniqueness, also laid the first groundwork
for Westernization.

These new currents among the Russian clergy appeared in the
1630s in the provinces and soon spread to the tsar's court. The
aim of the reformers was to bring the teachings of Christianity
closer to the people, to go beyond liturgy to convince the laity to
lead a Christian life. The reformers were mostly provincial parish priests, like the archpriest Avvakum, who came from a small
village near Nizhnii Novgorod. Eventually one of them, Stefan
Vonifat'ev, became Tsar Aleksei's spiritual father, which put the
reformers at the center of power. Known as the Zealots of Piety,
the reformers tried to reorganize popular religion. They tried to
repress drunkenness and even managed to convince the tsar to order the taverns closed on Sundays so that the congregation would
come to church sober. They also attempted to suppress the many
popular festivals attached to the observances of the Christian
year. For example, between Christmas and Epiphany (January 6)
the young people in the villages traditionally dressed up in cos-
tumes and went from house to house, begging for ritual gifts and
drinks. The reformers saw these traditions as interfering with a
true Christian life. All of this effort had no effect on popular custom, but showed the zeal of the reformers and won them favor at
court. The Zealots also tried to encourage preaching by the clergy.
Preaching required a new and more sophisticated learning from
the clergy, and to that end in 1649 the tsar began to invite Ukrai-

nian and Belorussian monks to Moscow to teach. These monks were the first important teachers of Western cultural traditions in Russia, and the consequences of their appearance were very great.

The desire for Western culture had come from inside Russia, but the new ideas came from abroad, from Poland. There the Orthodox church in Polish-ruled Belorussia and the Ukraine found itself part of a society with ties to West European culture. With the advent of the Renaissance, which spread to Poland by the sixteenth century, education and culture among the Polish ecclesiastical and secular elite moved toward Renaissance models. The Renaissance in Poland provided a cultural challenge to the Ukrainians along with the challenge of political and social domination. This challenge was rendered more acute by the church Union of Brest in 1596, in which the bishops of the Orthodox church in the Ukraine and Belorussia accepted the supremacy of the Pope. Unfortunately for the Uniates, as the supporters of Rome began to be known, the parish clergy and the laity refused to go along. The result was that the Orthodox church in the lands under Polish rule became illegal for the next thirty-five years, and in place of the hoped-for unity in religion increasingly violent discord spread. In spite of the relegalization of Orthodoxy in Poland in 1632, and the restoration of some of the churches to the Orthodox, the inferior status of the eastern church helped make Orthodoxy an increasingly plebeian religion in a society with growing social tensions. Social and religious tensions together were behind the massive revolt of Ukrainian Cossacks and peasants under Hetman Khmel'nyts'kyi in 1648.

In the meantime, the Orthodox church in the Ukraine and Belorussia responded to the cultural challenge by beginning to imitate European models, especially by the foundation of the Kievan Academy in 1632, under the sponsorship of Petro Mohyla, the Orthodox metropolitan of Kiev. The Kievan Academy taught its pupils in Latin, and taught them Polish and Greek as well. The curriculum, based on the post-Renaissance rhetoric and Aristotelian

philosophy, was exactly the same as in Western European schools.
In particular, the model for the Kievan Academy was the Jesuit
academies of Poland and other countries farther west. Thus by
1650 a whole new generation of Ukrainian and Belorussian clergy
emerged, Orthodox in faith but learned in the culture of Renaissance and Baroque Europe. It was these learned monks whom tsar
Aleksei called to Moscow starting in 1649.

The Ukrainian and Belorussian monks in Moscow brought a
new cultural world to the Orthodox church in Russia, at least at
the court and in Moscow. They added to the traditional celebration of the liturgy the regular practice of preaching and tried to
stress more fully the moral content of Christianity. They also insisted that a complete comprehension of the faith required learning, and by that they meant not merely extensive reading of the
fathers in Slavonic translation but also the Western learning they
had acquired in Kiev. They began to teach Latin and Polish, at
first primarily to the children of the chancery secretaries.

The most important of them, Simeon Polotskii (1629–1680),
was the teacher of Tsarevich Aleksei Alekseevich, until his death
in 1670 the heir to the Russian throne. Simeon was born in the Belorussian town of Polotsk, apparently the son of townsmen, merchants or prosperous artisans. He attended the Kievan Academy
and then the Jesuit academy in Wilno, learning Latin and Polish
to perfection as well as Slavonic. He then returned to Polotsk and
taught in the local Orthodox school. In 1656 and 1660 he wrote
poems to greet Tsar Aleksei, whose armies were occupying Polotsk, as the hero of Orthodox piety, rewarded by God for victory.
Routine in Western Europe, such verse was very new to the Russians. As Poland recovered strength in the 1660s, Simeon realized
that the return of Polish rule would spell the end of Orthodoxy in
Polotsk, so he left for Moscow in 1664, remaining there until his
death. In Moscow he composed much poetry and drama for court
occasions in the peculiar Slavonic of the seventeenth century,
undoubtedly stiff and exotic to the Russian reader but certainly

fully understandable. He also preached frequently, following the earlier Ukrainian preachers in stressing morality and learning as well as piety. His vast compilations of sermons were printed and even began to circulate outside of court circles. All of this activity took place in and around the court. He taught his pupils in the Zaikonospasskii Monastery across Red Square from the Kremlin, and preached in the Kremlin churches and monasteries as well as other churches in the center of the city. Many of his sermons were delivered on occasions when the whole court was present, major festivals of the Christian year or the funerals of important churchmen and dignitaries. His chief patron seems to have been Bogdan Khitrovo, who controlled the palace chanceries and was one of the few important officials not to be simply a client of Artamon Matveev, but another favorite in his own right. Simeon was particularly in favor under Tsar Fyodor (1676–82), when he was allowed to set up his own printing press. Simeon was both an influential figure and typical of the new culture of the later seventeenth century in Russia. His writings continued to be read well into the eighteenth century.

The movement for church reform in Russia not only gave a powerful impulse to interest in Western culture, it also produced a reaction to these Westernizing impulses in the form of a schism of the church, the schism of the Old Believers. The origin of the schism lay in the belief of the Zealots of Piety that many of the liturgical practices of the Orthodox Church in Russia were incorrect, and that the Russian Church had lost the original and true Greek practices. Patriarch Iosif had resisted all this change, but on his death in 1652, through the efforts of Vonifat'ev and Tsar Aleksei, the new Patriarch Nikon came from the ranks of the reformers. Nikon was serious about correcting the liturgy, and in spring 1653, he ordered that Orthodox Christians cross themselves with three fingers and made some changes in the liturgy. Years later, Avvakum remembered that when he saw the orders, "we saw that winter was coming, our hearts froze and our legs

trembled." Nikon's fellow reformers split, many of them refus-
ing to go along with the changes. The actual changes seem trivial
today, one of the most important being the sign of the cross,
whether it should be made with three fingers (Nikon's position)
or two (Avvakum's position).[3]

The opposition to Nikon's reforms produced a schism, the
first serious split in the Orthodox Church in Russia, and the first
example of wide-spread resistance to its authority. Nikon's opponents, who came to be known as Old Believers, were quickly
sent into exile in Siberia and elsewhere. Perhaps Nikon's liturgical reforms would have created less opposition if his own fate
had been easier. He was the absolute master of the church, and
soon created enemies by his autocratic ways. He was also very
powerful at court, and began to offend the boyars and eventually
the tsar himself. Already in 1658 there was a break: At one of the
court ceremonies a servant of Nikon's received what the patriarch
considered a slight. In a huff he announced that he was leaving his
duties and retired to the Monastery of the New Jerusalem west of
Moscow. Tsar Aleksei was unable to recall him, and the church
was without its head until 1666–67. In that year Tsar Aleksei
called a church council, which simultaneously deposed Nikon and
condemned Avvakum and other Old Believers.[4]

The church answered the challenge of the Old Believers in
large part by asserting that it was the lack of learning on the part
of the schismatics that had led them astray. That response by the
church was the core of the main reply to their charges, the *Rod
of Governance*, printed in 1669 and written by Simeon Polotskii.
The work was based on Simeon's Western education, and dem-
onstrated once again that church and state in Russia could no
longer continue to function effectively without borrowing from
the West. The effect of the schism in the church on the process of
Westernization was contradictory. It created in the population a
large minority hostile to any innovation in the church or in Russian culture and provided a basis for much of the popular hostil-

ity to Peter's reforms. At the same time, it also provided another impulse to the process of Westernization in the church at the level of the church and court elite.

As these new currents in religion and the ideas of Western learning were centered in the tsar's court, they naturally affected the boyar elite as well as the members of the ruling dynasty. Some of the boyars, the Princes Odoevskii, for example, were attracted by the new culture from Kiev even before 1649. Sometime in the 1650s or 1660s, the Princes Romodanovskii and Golitsyn began to teach their sons Latin and probably Polish as well. The new cultural elements appeared outside the elite. While still an unknown provincial officer's daughter, Peter's mother, Natalia Naryshkina, was brought up "in the Polish manner," that is with Western dress and the greater freedom of Western noblewomen. Artamon Matveev, well before he became the tsar's favorite and principal minister, had an interest in Western culture, and found a tutor to instruct his son in Latin and Polish. During his period of power he was the patron and organizer of the court theater, which produced Baroque dramas of virtuous kings and princesses based on biblical stories, performed by the boys of the German school in Moscow. Western styles of painting came to Russia, and even a bit of knowledge of Western science. Tsar Aleksei asked the Danish ambassador for a "tube like that of Tycho Brahe," the famous Danish astronomer. In other words, he wanted a telescope. (Ironically, Brahe was the last important astronomer to work without a telescope, an instrument first used by Galileo.)

POLITICAL THOUGHT

Ultimately the Westernization of Russian culture would have a massive impact on Russian political thought and values, but until well into Peter's reign this was not the case. The absence of any secular culture had profound consequences for traditional Russian political thought. Before Peter's time, Russians understood what we call political events and structures in moral terms derived from Orthodox Christianity. They did not ask the questions posed by classical and Renaissance political thought, such as where does sovereignty come from? Or what is the just state? They did not use the terms derived from classical antiquity: "monarchy," "aristocracy," "democracy." They assumed that the state was a monarchy and the most important issue to them was the moral action of the ruler.[5] Both tsar and boyars accepted the notion that the most important feature of the good state was the harmony of ruler and subjects, especially the ruler and his more powerful subjects. True piety on both sides would lead to just behavior, and thus ensure a harmony of justice. The tsar needed to be strong, but to act in consultation with his subjects, at least the powerful ones. The boyars in turn owed loyalty, service, and good counsel to the tsar. For the boyar as well as tsar, the greatest crime was to put his personal desires above the good of the whole. Among the boyars, that would lead to the sort of rivalries that gave rise to the Time of Troubles, and in the case of the tsar, would lead him to become a tyrant, the *tsar'-muchitel'* (the oppressor tsar) of legend.

The chief writings that touched on politics in the sixteenth century reflected these assumptions. In the 1560s Tsar Ivan the Terrible and Prince Andrei Kurbskii exchanged polemical epistles on Ivan's repression of his opponents during the Oprichnina. Kurbskii reproached him for not listening to wise counsel and executing those who only did their duty. Ivan replied by asserting that their counsel was not wise and that they harbored thoughts of treachery. Kurbskii did not make an argument for either personal or aristocratic rights, much less constitutionalism. He remained in the moral realm and argued that Ivan's victims were innocent. By implication, if they were guilty as Ivan believed, then his actions would be justified. Ivan also made no argument for secular absolutism: He argued that his power was from God and those that he executed had been guilty of disloyalty, so he was right to execute them.

These ideas did not change in the seventeenth century. There were still no political tracts, but indirectly the Russians wrote about politics in their historical works. The ideal was still the moral harmony of tsar and subjects, where the just tsar ruled in harmony with the pious people. Tsars not in harmony with the people were always bad, like Boris Godunov (curiously enough not Ivan the Terrible). The Russians could not conceive of the good monarch who ruled absolutely, indifferent to the views of his subjects, as advocated by European theorists of strong monarchy. They did not bother themselves with proving that the monarch was above the secular law, for their conception of law was essentially religious, the law of God. The tsar was not above the law of God, and that was the only law that counted. Religious traditionalism of this sort had no room either for secular absolutism or for aristocratic constitutionalism.

This tradition held into the second half of the century: Tsar Aleksei in his correspondence with his boyars held fast to the ideal of mutual harmony. Matveev's court theater provides another example, for Tsar Aleksei and the boyars attended all the performances and the plays depicted the kings and queens of ancient Israel and the Near East, images of good and bad monarchs. The biblical plays, in spite of their Western Baroque form, went little beyond the Russian tradition in their political content. In them some of the characters spoke for a seemingly secularized notion of the welfare of the people that the monarch should uphold, but the idea was so general that it fitted easily into an Orthodox Christian framework of piety and Christian virtues. The stories revolved around the virtue and wisdom (or lack thereof) of the monarch and his good and evil counselors. This emphasis on the ruler's virtue came from the European Baroque theater as well as from Russian tradition, so an element of Europeanization was certainly present, but muted by its adaptation to Russian circumstances. The same combination was visible in the poetry and orations that Simeon Polotskii composed for such court occasions as marriages and the accession of the tsar to the throne. In Western fashion he proclaimed the glory and power of the tsar, but also his piety and virtue. Both the theater and the poetry were also confined to a narrow circle at court, known only to the elite of court and church. Simeon provided a new image of the ruler, but modern political theory, that of the Renaissance and after, was as yet totally unknown in Russia.

All of these ideas about politics were also reflected in the houses and palaces of the tsars and the boyars. The royal palaces of Europe and Russia were not just places to live, but also a visual statement of the prevailing ideologies. From the Renaissance on, royal palaces in Western Europe were designed both to be esthetically beautiful and to glorify the monarch and celebrate his political and military success. Ceiling paintings were allegories of glory, and statues of Mars and Jupiter adorned the rooms and the gardens. More directly, pictures, murals, and tapestries depicted the king's victories and those of his ancestors. Sometimes they depicted his wisdom and justice, even his piety, but all that was much less important than the parade of military glory.

The palace of the Russian tsars in the Kremlin, on the other hand, was a different story. The palace lacked any of the basic attributes of Renaissance architecture—symmetry, classical decorative elements like Roman columns—and more important, presented a different message. Piety and justice, not military glory, were the theme of the wall paintings in the Kremlin palace, those that decorated the two main audience and meeting rooms in the Golden House (destroyed in the eighteenth century) or the Hall of Facets (still extant). The walls showed Christ ruling the world, with only a few portraits of Russian princes, such as Prince Vladimir of Kiev who introduced Christianity. The Russian princes were minor players in the overall scheme of Christianity, and had correspondingly minor places in the murals. The only military reference was Joshua's conquest of Canaan, supposedly alluding to the Russian conquest of Kazan'. In typical old Russian fashion, it glorified the victory of faith, not the tsar. Farther into the interior of the palace, in the private rooms of the ruling family, the decoration was similar: the life of Christ and other scenes. Boyar houses, what little we know of them, were no different, only smaller.

The ceremonial of the courts had the same function as the artistic scheme of the palaces. From the end of the Middle Ages European courts evolved an elaborate ceremonial designed to demonstrate the importance of the king. Some of these ceremonies took place at the court, pageants with all the trappings of late medieval and Renaissance art designed to show the monarch's valor and other kingly virtues. The entrance of the king into a major town was the occasion for similar ceremonies, as were annual events like the king's birthday or the anniversary of his accession to the throne.

In Old Russia, none of this existed. On the tsar's name day, he and the court went to church and prayed to his patron saint. The two great public ceremonies were the Palm Sunday procession and the Blessing of the Waters at Epiphany. Both of these ceremonies seem to have originated shortly after 1500 and remained central to the public display of the monarchy until Peter's time. On Palm Sunday the tsar led the metropolitan/patriarch of Moscow, seated on a donkey, through the Kremlin and across Red Square to the Cathedral of the Intercession ("Saint Basil's"). The patriarch played the role of Christ during His entry into Jerusalem in the days before the crucifixion, and the tsar showed his respect for the patriarch as head of the church and image of Christ. During Epiphany, the custom was to cut a hole in the ice on the Moscow River, where the patriarch, the tsar, and the people assembled. The patriarch then blessed the water and sprinkled the tsar and people with it, in remembrance of the baptism of Christ by Saint John the Baptist. During the ceremony the patriarch was again the center of the action, with the tsar showing his respect by word and gesture.

At the coronation of the Russian tsars the Russians took the Byzantine ceremony, with its exclusive emphasis on the power and glory of the emperor, and added a speech by the patriarch enjoining virtue and piety on the ruler. Most Russian court ceremonies departed from Byzantine precedents by reinforcing the role of the church and demonstrating visually and verbally the tsar's respect for the clergy. In all these ceremonies the boyars were the principal attendants and spectators, so they too participated in the public display of the tsar's piety and shared it.

THE END OF THE CENTURY

In the 1680s and 1690s the pace of cultural change quickened. Perhaps the most dramatic example is in church building, the period of the so-called Moscow or Naryshkin Baroque. There are only about a dozen examples of such churches in and around Moscow, all of them with similar characteristics. They departed from the traditional Russian churches in two ways. First, the overall structure was much freer in design, producing internal and external space that did not conform to the canons of older Russian church architecture. The new forms signified a break in more than just artistic style, for old Russian churches were more than just buildings set aside for worship. They were conceived as the meeting place of the divine and human worlds, the place where God manifested himself to men. Their form was not arbitrary, for it reflected this idea, the cupola on the top being round like the heavens as it was closer to God. The frescoes on the interior walls also illustrated the hierarchy of the cosmos. The new forms of the churches broke up this traditional order. Second, the new decorative schemes imported in massive quantity the styles of Baroque Central Europe and Poland, carved angels and gilded roundels. These even affected the iconostasis, another element of the old Russian Church with theological significance. The icon screen was the visible sign of the "deification" of the world, the manifestation of God in the world by Christ. Since about 1400 the old Russian icon screen had been fixed in the order and placing of the icons, but the new churches frequently ignored that tradition. The new style was visible in churches built on the orders of Tsarevna Sofia, the regent and Peter's antagonist, such as the Novodevichii Convent in Moscow. It was also the preferred style of Peter's supporters, his Naryshkin relatives (Fili) and Prince Boris Golitsyn (Dubrovitsy) or the Sheremetevs in their house church. The Naryshkin Baroque was a break both in architecture and in theology.

Many of the new churches were built by artisans trained in Poland, and the end of the seventeenth century was the period of the greatest influence of Polish culture. Important works of Polish literature were translated into Russian, and the language seems to have been widely known also. Perhaps partly because of its importance in Poland as well, Latin also had acquired some currency among the elite, more as a modern foreign language than for the classics. Simeon Polotskii and other Kievan monks had taught Latin as well as Polish, and the Likhudes taught some aristocratic students at the Slavo-Greco-Latin Academy as well. Prince Boris Golitsyn spoke to the Danish ambassador in Latin in 1684 and must have learned it from a tutor, since he went to no known school.

The death of Tsar Fyodor in 1682 had no effect on the spread of Westernization. Sofia and her de facto prime minister Prince V. V. Golitsyn patronized the scholars whom Simeon Polotskii had taught, and the prince had one of the largest known libraries of Western books in Russia in the 1680s. The new ideas continued to spread in the church. Patriarch Ioakim (1674–90), often portrayed wrongly as a reactionary, encouraged his own version of the new ideas. Disturbed by the possibility that relying on Polish-trained scholars might lead to Catholic influence, he imported Greeks to Moscow whom he believed were true to Orthodoxy. The Greek

Likhudes brothers, who arrived in Moscow in 1685, were given
the task of establishing the first real higher school in Moscow, the
Slavo-Greco-Latin Academy. In the new school, housed in the
monastery across from Red Square where Simeon Polotskii had
taught, they instructed the children of boyars as well as those of
the clergy and the government's secretaries. The Likhudes did not
bring "Byzantine tradition" to Russia: They taught in Latin and
were products of Italian schools in Padua. Their curriculum was,
if possible, even more Western than that of the Kievan Academy,
for they taught from Jesuit textbooks of logic, astronomy, rhetoric, and Aristotelian philosophy. Paradoxically, Ioakim supported
them in all their endeavors.

The Westernizing influence of Poland and the Ukrainian clergy
was reinforced by an entirely different element: the German suburb, located to the east of Moscow since the 1650s, and based
on earlier settlements of foreign merchants and soldiers. By the
1690s the German settlement had two thousand inhabitants, with
Lutheran and Reformed churches (the Russians prohibited Catholic churches until 1684), and schools to teach the children. There
were many Scots, Englishmen, and Dutch besides the Germans,
but the predominant language was German. Besides the many
merchants and their agents, numerous mercenary officers who
served in the Russian army, commanding infantry and European-
style cavalry regiments, lived in the German suburb. Though the
Germans provided the script and actors for Matveev's court theater, the real influence of the German suburb came later, after the
1680s. In part the reason was that Peter himself began to spend
much of his time there after about 1685.

The German suburb offered less in the way of literary culture and philosophical learning than the Ukrainian clergy or the
Likhudes, but it did offer some practical examples of Western
life and a great deal of military sciences. The mercenary officers
knew not only the new weapons and drill but also fortification and
artillery, both of which required much more mathematics than

any Russian possessed. Peter's great friend in the
was General Patrick Gordon, a Catholic Scot
a specialist precisely in fortification and artillery. Peter
navigation from Frans Timmerman, a Dutch merchant with an
interest in astronomy. Not surprisingly Peter's surviving school
notebooks are mostly mathematical and astronomical. All of this
introduced Peter and his entourage to engineering and technology of which they previously knew nothing. Peter moved on to
a fascination with waterworks, dikes, and sluices, and ships and
shipbuilding, both enthusiasms that found no echo at all among
the boyars. They did learn the new military practices, essential
as most of them were going to serve in the army and needed to
know them as the Russian military gradually changed from the
traditional cavalry to a European, largely infantry army equipped
with muskets.

The 1690s saw new trends at the court. Peter's mother died in
1694, and from then on he began to rule in his own right. In the
cultural arena, the result was an instant change in the ceremonial
of court, for Peter simply abandoned it. On Palm Sunday of that
year he omitted the procession, which he continued to omit for
the rest of his life. Boyars took the role played earlier by the tsar.
Similarly he ignored the Epiphany ceremony, coming (if at all) in
the role of a private soldier, standing with his unit away from the
action. He ceased the endless round of attendance at the liturgies
of the Kremlin cathedrals, and abandoned the palace for his modest wooden house in the suburban village of Preobrazhenskoe,
the headquarters of his new guards regiment. The Kremlin palace
gradually emptied out, leaving only apartments for his aged aunts
and a few other relatives.

Peter's first victory, the capture of Azov in 1696, brought another new element to the public ceremonial of the court. For the
first time military glory, not piety, was the theme of public celebration. Peter and his secretary, one Andrei Vinius, a Russified
Dutchman, created a grand entrance for the tsar and the returning

Russian army on European Baroque models, complete with arches of triumph on the Roman pattern. The arches had statues of Roman gods and mottoes derived from antiquity, such as Julius Caesar's "Veni, vidi, vici" (I came, I saw, I conquered), translated into Slavonic. Though the victory was one over the "infidel," the Islamic Turks, the theme of victorious Christianity was buried under the praise of military glory, of Russia, and of its young tsar. The new conception of the tsar was displayed for all to see.

The culmination of the previous decades of change and the spark to further cultural transformation was Peter's trip to Europe in 1697–98. The effect was so great partly because Peter himself finally saw Europe, but also because simultaneously he sent some two hundred young noblemen to the West, many of the chamber *stol'niki*, the sons of the great families like Dolgorukii, Golitsyn, and Kurakin. Peter himself followed his own interests, spending enough time working as a ship's carpenter in Zaandam, near Amsterdam, to qualify as a master. He then went on to examine the English shipyards at Deptford because he thought the Dutch lacked the necessary mathematical rigor in their building. He was fascinated by the many collections of exotic plants and animals he found in the Netherlands, and in England went to the Greenwich observatory and talked to English mathematicians and astronomers. All of this was a scientific culture, however elementary on Peter's part, which had been utterly unknown in Russia. Peter's personal tastes and interests were far ahead of those of most of his countrymen.

The boyars' sons and other noblemen were more representative. They went to Venice and Amsterdam, and later to other European centers. The original groups in 1697 were to study navigation for the new navy, and some actually did. Others merely absorbed a foreign language and a general European culture, which they brought to bear in the years to come. All of the new impressions and ideas would transform Russia as the young men of 1697–98 and the tsar matured, learned more from books and

life, and put what they learned into practice. Tha
of the rest of Peter's reign, a process with both cult
cal consequences. Until the travel and study in E
process a much-needed push, Westernization had been gradual.
The impact of the West before that time was largely confined to
religion, philological learning, and military affairs. In all three
areas it was very incomplete and affected mainly court circles and
the elite. Cultural forms derived from the West had little impact
on the provincial gentry, much less the mass of the population.
On the other hand, the very concentration of cultural change at the
elite level meant that it was intimately tied to the larger political
changes and issues of Peter's reign.

NOTES

1. Maksim taught enough Greek to the young boyar Prince Petr
Ivanovich Shuiskii to send him a letter in that language, and the boyar
Prince Andrei Mikhailovich Kurbskii (c. 1528–83), the famous refugee
and opponent of Ivan the Terrible, claimed Maksim as his teacher. Just
what Kurbskii learned from Maksim is not clear, perhaps only a respect
for learning and a sense of a wider world. There were also a very few
Russian writers in the sixteenth century who knew something of ancient
Greek and Roman writers, such as the *okol'nichii* F. I. Karpov (died
1539–42).

2. Thus Byzantium had two cultures, one religious and the other
secular, and Russia received only the religious side.

3. The problem was that Avvakum and his followers saw liturgy as
a mystical re-creation of the life of Christ, and all actions of a Christian, even personal acts of piety like making the sign of the cross, as
a manifestation of the divine. Therefore any innovations in them were
by definition human alterations to the unchangeable divine essence.
Nikon and his followers thought of proper liturgy more as a memorial
to Christ's life, and as something to be discovered by learning and the
examination of texts.

4. Nikon went into exile in the northern Ferapontov Monastery, and died in 1681. Avvakum suffered a harsher fate, for he went to Pustozersk, a military fort north of the Arctic Circle, where he spent the years in an underground cell writing his autobiography and the theological works that defended his position. He was eventually burned at the stake in 1682, and many of his followers perished as well. The schism of the Old Believers spread rapidly in the succeeding decades, especially in the north, the Urals, and Siberia, as well as the remoter areas of central Russia. It gradually absorbed other streams of local discontent with the church. Many of its followers dealt with persecution from the state by mass suicide, locking themselves in wooden churches and setting them on fire. Some of the Old Believers thought that the end of the world was coming, and that the Romanov dynasty was a sort of collective Antichrist. It was overwhelmingly a plebeian movement, with few nobles, much less boyars, among its followers. Its importance lay in the challenge it made to the religious and political order of Russia, a challenge that continued to the Revolution of 1917.

5. In concentrating on the moral action of the ruler medieval Russians shared some common culture with the West. In the medieval West the Aristotelian conception of the state taught in the universities by scholastic philosophers coexisted with a more popular conception of the state, which also revolved around the moral action of the king. This was the subject matter of the vast literature called the "Mirror of Princes." There is no evidence that the Russians knew any of the Western texts of this type.

FURTHER READING

Bushkovitch, Paul. "Cultural Change among the Russian Boyars 1650–1680: New Sources and Old Problems," *Forschungen zur osteuropäischen Geschichte* 36 (2000): 91–112.

———. "The Epiphany Ceremony of the Russian Court in the Sixteenth and Seventeenth Centuries," *Russian Review* 49 (1990): 1–18.

———. "The Formation of a National Consciousness in Early Modern Russia," *Harvard Ukrainian Studies* X, nos. 3/4 (December 1986): 369–73.

———. *Religion and Society in Russia: The Sixteenth and Seventeenth Centuries*. New York: Oxford University Press, 1992.

Chrissidis, Nikolaos A. *An Academy at the Court of the Tsars: Greek Scholars and Jesuit Education in Early Modern Russia*. DeKalb: Northern Illinois Press, 2015.

Cracraft, James. *The Petrine Revolution in Russian Architecture*. Chicago: University of Chicago Press, 1988.

Crummey, Robert O. "Court Spectacles in Seventeenth Century Russia: Illusion and Reality," in *Essays in Honor of A. A. Zimin*, ed. Daniel Waugh. Columbus, OH: Slavica, 1985, 130–58.

Flier, Michael S. "Breaking the Code: The Image of the Tsar in the Muscovite Palm Sunday Ritual," in *Medieval Russian Culture*, vol. 2, ed. Michael S. Flier and Daniel Rowland. Berkeley: University of California Press, 1994, 213–42.

Hippisley, Anthony. *The Poetic Style of Simeon Polotsky*. Birmingham, UK: Department of Russian Language and Literature, University of Birmingham, 1985.

Kollmann, Nancy Shields. *By Honor Bound: State and Society in Early Modern Russia*. Ithaca, NY: Cornell University Press, 1999.

Poe, Marshall. "What Did Russians Mean When They Called Themselves 'Slaves of the Tsar'?," *Slavic Review* 57, no. 3 (Fall 1998): 584–608.

Rowland, Daniel. "Did Muscovite Literary Ideology Place Limits on the Power of the Tsar (1540s–1680s)?," *Russian Review* 49 (1990): 125–55.

———. "Moscow—The Third Rome or the New Israel," *Russian Review* 55 (1996): 591–614.

Rowland, Daniel, "The Problem of Advice in Muscovite Tales about the Time of Troubles," *Russian History* 6, pt. 2 (1979): 259–83.

Weickhardt, George G., "Political Thought in Seventeenth Century Russia," *Russian History* 21, no. 3 (Fall 1994): 316–37.

Chapter Three

A Quarter-Century of Conflict, 1676–1699

The last quarter of the seventeenth century saw a sharp departure from the peace at court that had marked the reigns of Michael and Aleksei. The death of Tsar Aleksei in January 1676 led within months to the fall of his favorite, Artamon Matveev, and a new regime under Tsar Fyodor.

Fyodor was the eldest surviving son of Tsar Aleksei and his first wife, Maria Miloslavskaia, and with the new tsar his mother's relatives naturally took on new significance at court. Peter was not even the closest possible heir, for Fyodor had a younger brother Ivan, also Maria's son, who stood ahead of Peter in the line of succession. In this situation Peter, his mother, Natalia, and her Naryshkin relatives were bound to slip into the background. The fall of Matveev, however, complicated matters greatly, for it led to an attack on Matveev's Naryshkin allies, a conflict of a ferocity unseen at the Russian court since the Time of Troubles.

Out of the conflicts of those early months of 1676 came the rivalry of the Naryshkins and Miloslavskiis, the families of the two wives of Tsar Aleksei. In 1682 the Miloslavskiis were able to use the revolt of the musketeers who killed several of the Naryshkins and their allies, and seemingly come to power in the regency of Tsarevna Sofia over the boy tsars Ivan and Peter. Peter was able to overthrow Sofia in 1689, establishing himself on the throne and surrounding himself with his boyar allies. The result was not a return to the old balance of factions under the tsar, however, for Peter had larger plans and saw the boyar factions as an obstacle. He soon tried to rule alone, aided only by his favorites.

DISSENSION AND STRIFE

Contrary to legend, a Miloslavskii and Naryshkin faction did not exist when Tsar Aleksei died. There are no contemporary references to such factions at court, which is understandable: The Naryshkins had just joined the court and the Miloslavskiis were too far away. The immediate result of Aleksei's death was the proclamation of his son and heir Fyodor as tsar, but the new tsar was only fifteen years old and already dangerously ill from scurvy. The boyars, neglected under the Matveev ascendancy, held the reins of power, and they proceeded to fill the Duma with many new members, both from old Duma families and with new families from lower ranks in the nobility. By June Matveev had already lost many of his offices and in July, completely outmaneuvered, he was sent into exile as governor of Verkotur'e in the Urals. The boyars also tried to undo many of the cultural innovations of the previous reign, closing the court theater and talking of a general return to the old ways. In this early phase, the boyars as a whole, not any one grouping or clan, seem to have worked together to depose him.

Matveev's exile was not enough for his enemies. Tsarevna Irina, his old nemesis, and the Miloslavskiis now had free rein with a young and sickly tsar and a Duma filled with the enemies of the erstwhile favorite. A messenger soon caught up with Matveev and informed him that he was charged with sorcery and proceeded to search his baggage and that of his companions. The charges were murky and not all the records have survived, but it seems that one of the surgeons of the Apothecary Chancellery (the tsar's personal medical service), which Matveev had headed, charged him with reading books of magic. Matveev claimed it was actually an astrological treatise and had nothing to do with magic. After many of his servants and many witnesses were interrogated under rib-crushing torture, from which many died, nothing could be proven. He was sentenced to lose his rank of boyar, to lose his estate, and to go into a real exile in Pustozersk in the far north, where the Old Believers also languished.

Still the Naryshkins were not crushed. In December charges were found against them, asserting that Natalia's brothers had spoken of killing Tsar Fyodor. The same torture followed, but again nothing could be proven: Either they had said nothing of the kind or it was a misunderstanding. This time Natalia herself stepped in, demanding an audience with Irina and complaining that the Miloslavskiis were out to destroy her family. The boyars were no longer so enthusiastic and united. Prince Iurii Alekseevich Dolgorukii, one of the older boyars, an important general, and an opponent of Matveev in former times, spoke against continuing the investigation. Irina put an end to it, calling off the Miloslavskiis and sending the Naryshkin brothers into exile, but only to their country estates. The Miloslavskiis and Irina had triumphed, many innocent people were dead, but Matveev and the Naryshkins were still alive. They could wait.

Their return to favor took the next five years, for only Tsar Fyodor could bring it about and he needed first to emancipate himself. Quietly he began to form a circle of his own favorites from his household, the new boyar Ivan Iazykov and the Likhachev brothers Mikhail and Aleksei, all from lesser noble families. It helped him considerably that Tsarevna Irina died in 1679, and he immediately made plans to get married. His choice was Agafia Grushetskaia, from a very provincial noble family, but a girl raised to appreciate foreign ways. Among Fyodor's first acts after the marriage was to change the court costume, simplifying and regularizing it. His wife sometimes appeared in "Polish" dress. Unfortunately she died in childbirth the next year, but Fyodor, struggling with increasing ill health, did not stop. Impressed by the continued difficulties that the precedence system made for the army, he ordered it abolished on November 24, 1681,[1] after having consulted the Boyar Duma and the higher clergy. Two weeks later he also ordered Prince V. V. Golitsyn and the other boyars to investigate the needs of the army and for that purpose to call together representatives of the lower military ranks to give at least the appearance of consultation. When the Boyar Duma and the assembly agreed to reform the army, the tsar ordered a list to be drawn up of the personnel of the army. In the records of the decisions of the assembly of military ranks, the story is that they and the boyars then petitioned the tsar, pointing out that in such a list many great families would be absent since there were young sons not yet mature enough for such service: the Trubetskois, Odoevskiis, Kurakins, Repnins, Sheins, Troekurovs, Lobanov-Rostovskiis, and Romodanovskiis. To avoid this problem they proposed eliminating the whole precedence system. In reality the tsar had already done this, but the government wanted the act to appear as the result of the petition of the tsar's subjects. Thus, with Patriarch Ioakim and the boyars present in the Kremlin palace on January 12, 1682, Tsar Fyodor ordered the military records chancellery, the *Razriad*, to burn the records of the old system. New genealogical books would be compiled to record the greatness of the aristocratic families. Besides the tsar himself, the real authors of the measure seem to have been Fyodor's favorites, Iazykov and the Likhachevs. Prince Vasilii Vasil'evich Golitsyn, as aristocratic as anyone could be in Russia and a new favorite, also played a major role. The abolition of precedence did not in any way demote the boyar aristocracy, for they remained as before in all the key positions in the army and the state. What it did was to change the form of their service, and unlock it from the details of the service of their ancestors, providing a more flexible system of promotion and service, a more modern system that benefited the tsar and the aristocrats alike.

After this major decree was safely enacted, Fyodor decided to marry again and to recall Matveev and the Naryshkins. In February 1682, he married Marfa Apraksina, a young woman from a provincial noble family, not great boyars. He allowed Matveev to return from the north to his estate near Moscow, and the return of the Naryshkins seemed imminent. In a few weeks, however, Tsar Fyodor was dead. He had no children, and the only heirs were the ten-year-old Peter and his fifteen-year-old half-brother Ivan, partly blind and suffering from other ailments as well. Patriarch Ioakim summoned the boyars and the clergy the very day of Fyodor's death, April 27. After a brief discussion they chose Peter and proclaimed him the tsar. Ivan, the son of Maria Miloslavskaia, was set aside. His Miloslavskii relatives were not happy at the outcome.

Peter's reign as sole boy tsar lasted only a few weeks. While the selection of the tsar was proceeding in the Kremlin, trouble was brewing among the musketeers. The musketeers (*strel'tsy*) still formed the main part of the garrison of Moscow. The musketeers were not landholders: They were drawn from the common people and though provided with flour, clothing, and weapons, they were expected to a large extent to support themselves. They worked as artisans and small merchants in the capital when not soldiering, but unlike city people, they paid no taxes as soldiers of the tsar. The musketeers were to a certain extent privileged. In 1682 there were twenty such regiments, most of them in Moscow. Until midcentury they had been a crucial part of the Russian army, but increasingly their archaic weaponry and tactics made them ineffective in battle. Tsar Aleksei had formed regular units on the European model with Scottish and German mercenary officers who introduced into Russia the new drill and tactics that had emerged from the Thirty Years' War, rendering the musketeers obsolete. In spite of their inferiority in modern battles, the musketeers guarded the Kremlin and expected appropriate treatment. Yet their officers used them as workmen for their own purposes and treated them as servants, and the result was revolt.

When the musketeers came to the Kremlin on May 15, as-
sembling in front of the palace to demand redress, some of them
began to shout for Tsar Ivan. The Miloslavskiis had planted their
agents, and a social revolt had come to the aid of a palace intrigue.
Ivan, Peter, and Sofia came out on the steps and Matveev tried
to reason with them. The musketeers immediately killed him and
Prince M. Iu. Dolgorukii, the son of the boyar and important general Prince Iu. A. Dolgorukii. The musketeers demanded Peter's
uncle, and when he appeared on the palace stairs threw him down
on the upturned pikes of the soldiers. Other Naryshkin relatives,
Prince Iu. A. Dolgorukii, one of the tsar's physicians, and many
others were also murdered. In these days the Naryshkins' allies
seem to have included many of the great families, not only the
Princes Dolgorukii but also the Odoevskiis, Romodanovskiis, and
the boyars Sheremetev, who had served the Moscow princes since
the fourteenth century. With the musketeers in control of the city,
however, aristocratic support was not enough. On May 23, 1682,
the musketeers came again to the Kremlin, asking Prince Ivan
Khovanskii, their new champion, to petition Tsarevna Sofia that
Ivan and Peter be made co-tsars. Again an assembly of dignitaries
met under Patriarch Ioakim and granted the request.

It was during the revolt that Tsarevna Sofia (1657–1704),
the daughter of Aleksei by Maria Miloslavskaia, came into the
picture. She began to negotiate with the musketeers and to play
an increasingly prominent role in politics. It may have been she
who arranged the compromise—the double election of Ivan and
Peter. Eventually it was Sofia who put an end to the disturbances.
She played her cards well, waiting over the summer for the right
moment. Prince Khovanskii had taken over leadership of the
musketeers, and Sofia not only wanted to calm the soldiers, she
also wanted to eradicate rivals. In September she had Khovanskii
and his son suddenly arrested and executed and afterward quickly
restored her own authority over the musketeers. Sofia was now
the regent of Russia.

The seven-year regency that followed saw no more great up-
heavals but plenty of intrigues and maneuvers. Normally historians see the period as the ascendancy of the Miloslavskiis, and
indeed Peter himself believed that family to have been his principal rivals for the rest of his life. In fact, the only Miloslavskii
with any power was Sofia herself. The male relatives of tsar Ivan
played no role: The senior man of the clan, Ivan Mikhailovich
Miloslavskii, had already lost all his offices mysteriously in May
1682. Only a few months after the consolidation of Sofia's power
he was still on the sidelines and vociferously angry about it. With
his death in 1684 no more Miloslavskiis played any major role.[2]
The real power rested with Sofia and Prince V. V. Golitsyn. They
gave many offices to his lesser clients (Narbekov, Rzhevskii) but
they also tried to maintain some balance and gave other offices
to the Naryshkin faction. One of the regency's most important
rivals and the chief supporter of the Naryshkins was Prince Boris
Alekseevich Golitsyn, the first cousin of Sofia's favorite. In this
case, as in so many others, even close members of the same family or clan did not agree. Sofia put Boris Golitsyn in charge of the
Kazan' Palace, an office of huge importance with control over
the whole of the middle and lower Volga basins and in charge
of relations with the nomadic native peoples of the southern and
southeastern border, the Tatars, Bashkirs, Kalmyks, Circassians,
and others. Sofia was trying to appease her opponents by compromise.

The leaders of the Naryshkin faction, Natalia herself, Boris
Golitsyn, and others plotted all sorts of intrigues against Sofia, but
to no avail. She had her greatest success in 1686 when she negotiated the "Eternal Peace" with Poland. The treaty gave Kiev to Russia, thus consolidating the gains of 1667, but also entered Russia
into an alliance with Poland, the Holy Roman Empire, Venice, and
the Papacy against the Ottoman Turks. The struggle against the
Turks had been a major goal of Russia since Ordin-Nashchokin's
time, including an inconclusive war that Tsar Fyodor had waged

in 1676–81 over the Dniepr fortress of Chigirin. Now Sofia had to follow up her treaty with action. Prince V. V. Golitsyn commanded her army, but the senior generals under him mostly were supporters of the Naryshkins.

This traditional policy of balancing factions, so much like Tsar Aleksei's before 1667, did not work. There were shouting matches in the Kremlin between Natalia and Sofia. One of Peter's principal supporters, the Circassian Prince Mikhail Alegukovich Cherkasskii, drew a knife during an argument with V. V. Golitsyn, and this during the annual court pilgrimage to the Trinity Monastery. More important, the 1687 campaign against the Crimean Khanate, Turkey's vassal, was an ignominious failure. Golitsyn's only success was to depose Ukrainian Hetman Ivan Samoilovich, a Naryshkin ally, in favor of the hopefully more compliant Ivan Mazepa.

Meanwhile, Peter and his faction went from strength to strength. In 1688 he began to attend the sessions of the Duma and listen to policy discussions. Early in 1689 he was married to Evdokiia Lopukhina, another young woman of lesser noble status, but one whose grandfather had served with Artamon Matveev and the Naryshkins in the *strel'tsy* in the 1660s. The family had followed the Naryshkins into court circles in the 1670s. Around this time the household of Tsar Ivan, led by Prince Petr Prozorovskii, Ivan's tutor, began to move to support Peter against Sofia. The regent was increasingly isolated, and all that was needed was another failure.

That failure came with the Crimean campaign of 1689, another disaster, where Golitsyn's army got as far as the northern approach to Crimea at Perekop, then turned around and left after inconclusive talks with the Tatars. Sofia wanted to treat Golitsyn's return as a triumph, but Peter refused to go along. Rumors spread that Sofia might try some sort of strike against Peter.

Peter was no longer a boy. Now seventeen, he had been spending much of his time at Preobrazhenskoe, a village outside of

Moscow, in a modest wooden house where he lived with his mother and his household. That household by 1689 had come to include a regiment of "play" (*poteshnye*) troops gathered from his servants, nobles and plebeians. With them he worked at military drill and target practice, military maneuvers, and capturing small fortresses. Not yet a force of much importance, they gave him at least a sense of confidence and put him in contact with real soldiers, like Scottish General Patrick Gordon, who had served in Russia for more than twenty years.

On the night of August 7, 1689, a group of soldiers heard in the streets of Moscow that Sofia was plotting with the musketeers to kill Peter. They rode out to Preobrazhenskoe and warned him. He took it completely seriously, riding off with only a few servants in the middle of the night to the Trinity Monastery. Prince Boris Golitsyn, his play regiments, and the household followed the next day. The result was a standoff: Peter demanded from Sofia to know what the musketeers were up to. Sofia tried to rally her supporters. Her efforts were to no avail, for Patriarch Ioakim went to Peter and stayed with him, along with some of the boyars. In a few days the mercenary officers under Gordon and the musketeers came out to the Trinity Monastery. Peter's suspicions focused on Fyodor Shaklovityi, the head of the Military Chancellery (*Razriad*), an old ally of Sofia. On September 7 she agreed to give him up and he was promptly interrogated and executed with a few followers. Peter did not want him executed, but Patriarch Ioakim insisted. Sofia's regency was over. Peter sent her to the Novodevichii Convent in Moscow, on which she had lavished so much of her estate. V. V. Golitsyn went into exile, from which he never returned, and Peter was now in power.

Why did Sofia fall from power and with such ease? The trigger for the chain of events was the failure of the Crimean campaigns, for it discredited her government. If she had been the legitimate ruler, she might have survived these checks, as Peter would later survive many defeats. Sofia, however, was ruling only in the

name of her brother and half-brother. Furthermore, most important boyars had come to oppose her or were neutral, offering her
no support. Prince Prozorovskii, for example, took the household
of Tsar Ivan away from Sofia, joining Peter some time during
August. The support of the church and the mercenary officers also
helped Peter, and finally the defection of Sofia's former allies, the
musketeers, played a major role in her defeat, for it removed the
only armed force she could count on. Here as well, the failure of
the Crimean campaigns, and the very hard conditions the Russian
troops endured, further undermined her position. Peter came to
power with the army and the great families behind him.

PETER ON THE THRONE

For the first few years Peter's government and his actions reflected his support in 1689. Sofia's adherents were sent to govern
distant provinces, and Peter's supporters took or kept the main
offices. The Swedish envoy agent reported, "The Boyar Lev
Kirillovich Naryshkin, Tsar Peter's uncle, is the most important
at the helm, and great flattery comes to him from high and low."
Lev Kirillovich was only twenty-five in 1689, and perhaps not the
most talented in the government. Years later Prince B. I. Kurakin,
who did not like Naryshkin or any of his faction, wrote that he
had mediocre intelligence and drank too much, but had to admit
that he was not a villain and often did good, if only on a whim.
Naryshkin's power was entirely informal. Prince Boris Golitsyn
remained at the Kazan' Palace, while Tikhon Streshnev took over
the army from Shaklovityi, and Prince Petr Prozorovskii received
the treasury offices. Russia's foreign policy was the charge of the
Duma secretary Emel'ian Ukraintsev and was not particularly
consistent, for Russia remained part of the Holy League, but did
no fighting. Rivalries among the boyars in Peter's government
made policymaking difficult. Boris Golitsyn and Lev Naryshkin

were particularly jealous of one another, and Streshnev had to adjudicate rivalries and insults between them and many others. In February 1692, an argument erupted between Prince Boris Golitsyn and Prince Iakov Dolgorukii. At one of the many banquets during Shrovetide, given by an unnamed Duma secretary at the palace, Prince Boris encouraged another guest to pull Prince Iakov's hair as a joke. Dolgorukii stabbed the joker with a fork and was believed to have killed him, with the result that both princes had to appear before the tsar the next day. Dolgorukii called Boris a drunk and said that "he would rather [Boris] could pull his father's beard than be able to pull his hair." The case went to Tikhon Streshnev, who found against the Dolgorukiis, Prince Iakov and his brother, fining them and ordering them as a humiliation to go to prison on foot. On the way they were recalled, evidently pardoned. The case dragged on until 1695, when Golitsyn forgave them the fine. Toward the end of 1692 another banquet at the house of P. V. Sheremetev ended in a quarrel in which Prince M. G. Romodanovskii called the boyar A. S. Shein a whore's son and Shein struck him. The case went this time not to Streshnev but to Boris Golitsyn, who ordered Romodanovskii to pay an enormous fine for dishonor.

While the boyars quarreled, Peter spent more and more time in Preobrazhenskoe with his soldiers. From 1691 at least the "play" regiment had become two guards regiments, the Preobrazhenskii and Semenovskii guards, which played a major role in the Russian army and politics. Like the earlier play regiments, their recruitment from his household meant that the sons of the highest aristocracy served in the guards. Peter's military pastimes became more and more professional under the guidance of Patrick Gordon. He spent much time in the German suburb, and met the Genevan-Swiss officer François Lefort, with whom he developed a close friendship. Lefort had become the tsar's favorite, and reinforced his influence by introducing Peter to Anna Mons, a German innkeeper's daughter. Mons became Peter's mistress, the first (known) mistress of a tsar in Russian history. Peter was also developing an intense interest in boats, soon to become a lifelong obsession. In 1688 he had found a small English sailing boat in a barn near Moscow and had it repaired so that he could sail it on Pleshcheevo Lake north of Moscow. From this experience he had learned about sailing, but he wanted to see the real sea. Russia's only port in those days was Archangel, far in the north at the mouth of the Dvina on the White Sea. In 1693 he and his friends and servants from Preobrazhenskoe made the long journey there, and even acquired a twelve-gun yacht, the *St. Peter*. Peter was not allowed to sail on the open sea, for his mother expressly forbade it. Natalia, however, did not have long to live, and when she died in January 1694, Peter was at last his own man.

The first step Peter made was to cease entirely to come to the Kremlin ceremonies. For the first time in centuries the tsar did not appear to lead the patriarch's donkey in the traditional procession on Palm Sunday. In the summer of 1694 he went to Archangel again and this time he put to sea in the *St. Peter*. When he returned in the fall to Moscow, Peter announced that Russia would take up the war again against the Turks, and this time in a different way. He ordered hundreds of carpenters and massive quantities of supplies assembled at Voronezh on the Don, and recruited Dutch ship carpenters to instruct them, for Peter was building a navy. What the boyars thought is not recorded, but he made them and the church, not just the peasantry, pay for the fleet.

By the spring of 1695 the fleet was ready, built at record speed with the personal participation of the tsar, who wanted to learn how to build with his own hands.[3] A combination of small sailing ships and oared galleys in the Mediterranean style, it sailed down the Don to the Turkish fortress of Azov at the mouth of the river, at the northeast corner of the Sea of Azov. Peter's idea was not only to help fight the Turks on a distant theater that they could not easily afford to defend, but also to gain access to the sea. The first siege, despite the presence of Lefort, Gordon, and other foreign experts, was not a success. Next year Peter returned, with his army under the command of the old boyar A. S. Shein, and there was better organization under him. This time the fort fell, and Peter's army returned to Moscow to a European-style triumphal entry. Only then did they go to church for a traditional service of thanksgiving.

Much more was afoot than new ceremonials. Peter decided to send a great embassy to Europe, headed by the new favorite Lefort. Second in rank after Lefort was the boyar Fyodor Golovin, who had just successfully negotiated the Treaty of Nerchinsk (1689) with the emperor of China.[4] The embassy was to consist of several hundred men, many of them "volunteers" going along to see Europe, including Peter himself going incognito, and many young Russian nobles. In the crowd was also a soldier in Peter's old "play" regiment, one Alexander Menshikov, the son of a servant in the tsar's stables. His rise to power was just beginning. The diplomatic aim of the embassy was to strengthen the alliance against the Ottomans, and for Peter personally it was to see the Dutch shippers and boatbuilders on their home territory. As he was leaving, Peter also dispatched a number of young Russian aristocrats to study foreign languages and navigation in Venice and Amsterdam. He was not the only one who was to learn from the West.

A new world was opening up in front of the Russian elite, but many of them were not happy with it. The most serious indication of such unhappiness was the plot discovered in February 1697. Several men of Duma rank, the *okol'nichii* Aleksei Sokovnin, his three sons, and the boyar Matvei Pushkin, had been talking with one of the musketeer colonels, Ivan Tsykler, about ways to replace Peter. They were discontented because Sokovnin and Pushkin had been passed over for promotion, and also were fearful when they learned that their sons would be sent abroad to learn new things.[5] Tsykler apparently disliked Peter's trip abroad and sympathized with the imprisoned Sofia. They all hoped to get rid of Peter in some way, perhaps by encouraging a new revolt among the musketeers. Sokovnin wanted to replace him with A. S. Shein, while Tsykler preferred the important boyar and general, B. P. Sheremetev, who was popular in the army. They talked of restoring Sofia, but Sokovnin rejected the idea, since he did not want the return of the tsarevna and her favorite V. V. Golitsyn either. The plotters did not get far enough to make concrete plans when they were discovered, but that was enough: Sokovnin, Pushkin, and Tsykler were executed. At their execution Peter ordered the body of the long dead Ivan Mikhailovich Miloslavskii exhumed and burned, for in his mind the Sokovnin–Tsykler plot was just another example of the effects of Miloslavskii intrigues.

Peter thought he could leave without fear of trouble at home, and so he left in March 1697, putting the principal boyars in charge. Prince F. Iu. Romodanovskii, the head of the Preobrazhenskii Chancellery—his personal office—and the administrator of the main guards regiment, was to look after order in Moscow. Peter regularly corresponded with his uncle L. K. Naryshkin, who kept an eye on diplomacy, as well as with Prince B. A. Golitsyn, A. S. Shein, and T. N. Streshnev. Peter also remained in close touch with the secretary Andrei Vinius, the son of a Dutch merchant whose family had remained in Russia. Vinius gave him a source outside the aristocracy. The whole arrangement was informal, as during the Azov campaigns: The boyars would run the country, with Romodanovskii as the principal contact with the tsar. The very informality of the arrangement suggests Peter's lack of concern with the abilities and motives of the elite. He would have cause to change his mind.

The first sign of trouble was the delay in accepting his decision to divorce his wife, Evdokiia. Apparently Peter took the decision on the eve of his departure, when he exiled to distant governorships several of his wife's Lopukhin relations. Exactly how she had displeased Peter is not known, but by spring 1698, he was writing to Lev Naryshkin and others, ordering them to convince her to accept his decision. Members of the Lopukhin family were naturally aghast, and even Peter's son and heir, Tsarevich Aleksei (1690–1718), accused Lev Naryshkin of plotting his mother's demise. Most of the boyars sympathized with Evdokiia, and Peter's allies dragged their feet. Even more important was the opposition of Patriarch Adrian (1690–1700), who was also angry with Peter for allowing the sale of tobacco and for excessive toleration of Catholics.[6] An even more important challenge came in the late spring of 1698. The musketeers along the Polish frontier, under the command of the aged Prince M. G. Romodanovskii, were bringing petitions to the capital alleging various forms of oppression and malfeasance. As the summer progressed, the musketeers moved toward the capital: The petitions had turned into open revolt. They got as far as the Monastery of the New Jerusalem several miles west of the capital, where the boyars had brought an army to meet them, under Patrick Gordon with the new-style regiments as well as the traditional gentry cavalry. A short encounter settled the issue, and the musketeers surrendered on June 18. Shein and the boyars had the leaders briefly interrogated, and then executed.

When the first news came, on July 15, Peter was in Vienna after a successful trip to England, where he examined English boatbuilding and naval maneuvers, talked to astronomers, and looked in on a Quaker meeting. In England he also had unpleasant news: The emperor wanted to make peace with the Turks, leaving Russia out on a limb. In the Habsburg capital Leopold assured him that he would help Peter make peace with the Ottomans, and the tsar knew that soon his hands would be free for other engagements. He left Vienna, deciding to skip Italy and move on to Saxony and Poland. Just the previous year, the Polish diet had elected Augustus, the elector of Saxony, as king of Poland. Augustus II ("the Strong") was a reasonably successful commander in war and a new-baked Catholic (to satisfy Polish requirements) with big ambitions. He wanted to take Livonia from Sweden, and needed Peter as an ally, especially after the Russian triumph at Azov. The letters from Moscow were urgent, so Peter met Augustus in Poland only briefly on his hurried return journey, but it was a meeting fraught with major consequences. The conversations of the two rulers laid the foundations for the Northern War, but for the moment it was only a distraction for the tsar from more serious business.

PETER'S RETURN

On Peter's return to Moscow he made his position clear. He went to visit his mistress, not his wife. He greeted his subjects with a new ceremonial: He kissed them all and embraced everyone.[7] He personally shaved the beards of Shein and Romodanovskii, and ordered other boyars to shave theirs. He went to see Patriarch Adrian to explain his position regarding his wife and soon sent her away to a convent. Peter also ordered several priests interrogated, for he was deeply suspicious of the church and believed that the clergy might have supported the musketeers. He also ordered the interrogation under torture of hundreds of musketeers.

Peter ordered such a wide-ranging investigation because he did not trust the boyars, especially when he learned of the rapid execution of the rebel leaders, and the opposition of Gordon and other generals to that decision. Peter was convinced that his half-sister Sofia was behind the revolt, and indeed he was able to confirm that some sort of messages had passed between the leaders, those executed before his return, and the tsarevna. He even went to confront her himself, but was able to learn very little. At several banquets that fall, where foreign diplomats were present, he flew into a rage at the boyars, accusing Shein of selling army positions for money. More seriously, he also accused them of harboring treacherous designs against his own person. Imperial Ambassador Ignaz von Guarient reported:

A few days ago at Lefort's he [Peter] said publicly as I stood by, "I am no tsar over men but over dogs and irrational beasts. And what even more afflicts my mind is that I must now clearly confess that for a long time they have not only tried to ruin me; and indeed they (except two or three) carry the inward spirit of disloyalty and hourly think how they could bring such a thing against me." The boyar Naryshkin who had to hear all this, said to the tsar, "My lord, why do you bother yourself now? With your command alone all this can be easily remedied. Give over and place your thoughts on the scales of justice: if you recognize among your subjects disloyalty then do not spare their blood." The tsar said, "Lord, it shall happen and be done well according to your own advice very soon."

In fact Peter did not open any investigation of boyar disloyalty, but he was also incensed at the rivalries among the boyars. At Christmas time one of the banquets turned into a shouting match between Naryshkin and Boris Golitsyn. Naryshkin, who was drunk, accused Golitsyn of bewitching the tsar to gain favor, and the prince replied that Naryshkin had always been disloyal and hungry to govern. The dispute enraged the tsar, who threw a glass of wine at Naryshkin's feet and pushed away Lefort when he tried to calm him. Peter left for Preobrazhenskoe in a towering rage and threatened both of them with the most serious punishment.

It was the musketeers who paid for these controversies. Peter ordered hundreds of executions, and made the boyars supervise the investigation and torture and carry out the sentences. They were fully involved in the repression of the rebellion. The execution of the rebels, however, was not the only occupation of that winter. Peter began to change his whole mode of government. Ambassador Guarient commented:

Above all the tsar finds daily, more and more, that in the whole empire not one of his blood relatives and boyars can be found to whom he can entrust an important office; he is therefore forced to take over the heavy burden of the empire himself, and pushing

back the boyars (whom he calls disloyal dogs) to put his hand to a
new and different government.

The changes began that January. Peter stripped Shein of his
position in the army. Peter then found new ways of raising revenue that circumvented the older administration hierarchy, where
the boyars played a major role. He decreed a new type of taxation
by ordering the population to address the government in petitions
and other matters only on paper with an official stamp, for which
they paid. This idea came from one Aleksei Kurbatov, a Catholic
convert, serf of B. P. Sheremetev, and anonymous proponent
of the scheme. Peter found out the authorship, and not only
adopted Kurbatov's scheme but also gave him a position in the
administration. Another reform of even greater importance was
the establishment of elected committees in most of the towns to
collect the major taxes on the urban population, the sales tax and
the assessment on property. The new citizen-administrators, with
the German title of *burmistry*, may not have had much power, but
their existence removed the collection of the Russian treasury's
most important cash income from under the control of the provincial governors, aristocrats, or ordinary nobleman.

Even more radical was his conduct of foreign policy, which
entirely sidelined the boyar elite. In the sixteenth and seventeenth
centuries the boyars had always played a major role in the conduct of foreign policy: Ambassadors from abroad traditionally
never saw the tsar privately, only in public audience. All major
embassies and negotiating sessions in Moscow involved several boyars as well as lesser folk. The Ambassadorial Office by
tradition was usually headed by a secretary, not a boyar, which
prevented one boyar from dominating foreign policy. The Boyar
Duma as a whole had a greater voice with a secretary in charge of
this office.[8] In the 1690s, the appointment of the Duma secretary
Ukraintsev continued the traditional system of entrusting foreign
affairs to a professional administrator rather than a boyar. Dur-

ing Peter's absence in 1697–98, his uncle seems to have been explicitly granted supervision of foreign affairs such as Peter could not handle from abroad. Until 1699, the traditional structure remained.

Peter's new manner of governance could not have been more different. During the trip to Europe he had already conducted the serious discussions with kings and ministers in person. The main issue before him now was the alliance that he had been offered by both Denmark and Poland against the then hegemonic power in northern Europe, Sweden. Both powers began to explore the issue with Peter while he was abroad, but early in 1699 Denmark began to press for a formal alliance. Both Lefort and Boris Golitsyn opposed the alliance and the whole scheme of war with Sweden. Lev Naryshkin, by contrast, was in favor of it and had even explained his position to the Danish ambassador, Paul Heins, several months before. Peter ignored both proponents and critics.

The tsar announced that he was going south to Voronezh to supervise the construction of the fleet, and he asked the Danish ambassador to accompany him, as well as Fyodor Golovin. He did not ask Lefort (who soon died in any case) or Lev Naryshkin. In Voronezh the tsar met with Heins secretly at night, in a wooden house with the doors locked, the shutters closed, and only Heins, Peter, Golovin, and the translators present. Early in 1699 they worked out the treaty, which committed Russia to go to war on the side of Denmark (and eventually Saxony-Poland) against Sweden. Peter agreed to move as soon as the ongoing negotiations with Turkey led to a truce or peace. He told Heins to keep the treaty and the discussions secret, and particularly not to tell any of the Russian boyars. Naryshkin, who had followed the tsar on his own account, could only guess what was happening and fume. The boyars did not find out that Peter had committed them to war until nearly the end of the year.

The coming war was crucial to Peter's plans, for above all he wanted a port on the Baltic. He was perfectly aware that the

Neva River and the surrounding terrain had recently belonged to Russia, but he also wanted a seaport that was not as distant from central Russia and from the European heartland as Archangel. Only by defeating Sweden could he reconquer the area, and consequently he eagerly responded to the overtures from Augustus II of Saxony-Poland and Denmark.[9] Peter wanted the port as a commercial port, for he was aware of the importance that trade was coming to have in Europe, and also as a shorter path to the West, a "window into Europe," in the later phrase of the poet Alexander Pushkin. He seems not to have cared what the aristocracy thought about these plans, other than to prevent any possible interference.

The gradual end of consultation with the boyars paralleled Peter's gradual abandonment of the old ranking system. After 1694 Peter made almost no appointments to the rank of boyar or any of the other Duma ranks. Soon there would be no Duma to consult. The boyars also had to endure mockery from Peter's court jester, who joked about their incompetence and laziness in the tsar's service in front of Swedish diplomats. They had already learned that they were to shave their beards and soon found out that they were to wear different clothes, for in the course of 1700 Peter decreed that the upper classes were to wear "Hungarian" and "French" dress. That meant the end of the long fur-trimmed robes (the kaftans) and the tall hats the boyars had worn for centuries. Now, like eighteenth-century Europeans, they were to wear short coats, knee-length pants, and stockings. In the next year Peter ordered the women as well to adopt Western dress, giving them until January 1, 1701. The aristocratic women in particular disliked the new dress, with garters to hold up the stockings, high-heeled shoes (a source of endless trouble), low necklines, and worst of all, uncovered hair.[10] Late in 1699, Peter also ordered Russia to go over to the Western dating of the year, starting from the birth of Christ rather than the presumed date of creation. The year 7202 became 1700. None of the boyars were consulted about any of this, and there was much grumbling, especially about the expense of the new wardrobes.

Another cultural change of momentous importance came partly by accident. In October 1700, Patriarch Adrian died. Adrian was hostile to the Catholic Church, less so to Protestants, but he was not just a traditionalist. If not particularly intellectual himself, he was surrounded by clergy who were and read the Western books that were coming into Moscow. Some even produced sermons and even poetry rather in the spirit of Simeon Polotskii. Be that as it may, the church was the center of the older Russian culture that Peter was determined to change. At the patriarch's death, he simply prevented the clergy from electing a successor. To administer the church, Peter chose Stefan Iavorskii, a Ukrainian abbot whose funeral sermon for General Shein had just impressed the tsar so much that he ordered Adrian to make him a bishop in Russia. Stefan found himself the bishop of Riazan', a town south of Moscow, and a few months later the patriarch died. Stefan was a product of the Kiev Academy, fluent in Latin and Polish as well as Slavonic, the sort of man that Peter, for the time, wanted to promote in the Russian church. His sermons continued to be popular with Moscow congregations. The church had always been involved in high politics in Russia, and Stefan would prove no different. Peter would come to regret the choice.

The cultural changes that these moves implied for the moment were overshadowed by the radical changes in the army. Since the boyars had traditionally provided the commanders and officers of the Russian army, these innovations affected every one of them. Together with Adam Weyde, a Russian general of German or Dutch origin, Peter produced an entirely new manual for training and drill. This was to be primarily an infantry army, drilled and trained according to European models. The European methods required the units to move and fight as a group in defined lines and squares of men, not just hurling themselves against the enemy.

Cavalry as well as infantry were to fight in formation as well, not in a crowd like the old gentry cavalry. Few Russian officers or nobles knew much about such tactics, only those who had served in the few new-style regiments or in Peter's "play" regiments, now converted into the two guards regiments the Preobrazhenskii and Semenovskii. Many officers knew nothing of the new styles of fighting. In addition Peter began to recruit men for the new regiments not only from the peasantry as before but also from house servants and surplus courtiers. None of these innovations were popular with the aristocracy.

Peter did not completely sideline the great families in forming the new army. The guards were aristocratic from their inception. He appointed Prince Iakov Dolgorukii to head the supply department, with the German title of *krigskommisar*. He continued to maintain some traditional gentry cavalry and put it under the command of B. P. Sheremetev, recently returned from Italy. Important commanders besides Weyde included A. M. Golovin, Prince I. Iu. Trubetskoi, and Prince N. I. Repnin, all impeccably aristocratic. They had served in the guards and hence understood the new tactics, but so had many others of less exalted origin whom Peter passed over for generals. Under these aristocratic generals were colonels and junior officers at first largely recruited among European mercenaries, but with time Russian nobles began to learn their profession and earn promotion. To the end of Peter's reign, however, the highest army commands remained in the hands of aristocrats. Peter did not want to consult the Boyar Duma but he did not pass over the aristocrats for important commands in the army.

The last thirty years of the seventeenth century in Russia were troubled years. Not only were there many instances of popular revolt and religious dissent, but the elite itself was torn by factional battles at court. When the two coincided, as in 1682, the consequences were grave for the court elite. The response of the tsars to these court rivalries was to try to stand above them with the aid of a favorite or favorites. Tsar Aleksei had Artamon Matveev; Tsar Fyodor had Iazykov, the Likhachevs, and Prince V. V. Golitsyn; while Sofia relied mainly on Golitsyn. Peter himself rapidly found first Lefort and then Golovin and Alexander Menshikov. The favorites were outside the networks of aristocratic rivalries and tended to consolidate the elite in opposition against them, as happened to Matveev in 1676 and Golitsyn in 1689. Nevertheless, Peter's predecessors had continued to work with the great aristocrats, appointing them to the major offices in government and the army. Peter was the first to try to break with that policy after his return from Europe in 1698. He left the great men in their offices, but increasingly created new structures that allowed him to go around them, either informal structures around the favorites or new structures such as those resulting from the reorganization of the army.

Peter's new policy was a revolution in government, for he ceased meeting with the Duma and began to make all the decisions with Golovin and a few others, lesser folk like the secretary Vinius, Kurbatov, and Menshikov. Menshikov was still the second favorite after Golovin, and was more of a drinking companion than a governmental figure. His only important positions were a junior rank in the Preobrazhenskii guards and supervisor of the education of Peter's heir, Tsarevich Aleksei Petrovich. Menshikov's meteoric rise was in the future.

The need for the new policy was twofold. Peter was sick of the internal rivalries among the elite and their general inability to do his will effectively and promptly. He did not exploit and increase the rivalries among the aristocrats to strengthen his power; he tried to suppress the rivalries, and when that failed, to go around their participants. The other reason was the aristocrats' attitude to him and his policies. Rightly or wrongly, he suspected them of covert opposition. They were unhappy about his divorce, many of his cultural innovations, the new military organization, and the expensive new navy. They were not opposed to everything Western. They were the same boyars who built churches in the new Western Baroque style, learned Polish and Latin, and even developed an interest in Western religions.

The breaking point came with the musketeer revolt of 1698 and the approaching war with Sweden. Peter suspected the boyars of concealing the true nature of the revolt, assuming that its real aim was to restore Sofia. This he could not tolerate. As the idea of joining with Denmark and Poland-Saxony against Sweden grew in his mind, he found that his closest supporters like Boris Golitsyn, and even the favorite Lefort, opposed him. He made the necessary treaties without consulting the boyars and then reorganized the army in such a way as to reward professional military competence, not merely aristocratic rank. In 1698–99 he believed that he could not modernize Russia with the boyar elite. He would soon learn that he could not modernize Russia without them either.

NOTES

1. All dates are Old Style only, unless both styles are given. Old Style dates refer to the Julian calendar, New Style to the Gregorian calendar.

2. Lesser Miloslavskiis continued to receive court and military appointments through the regency of Sofia and Peter's entire reign.

3. Peter also began to learn Dutch from the carpenters, as we know from his surviving vocabulary lists. He perfected it later in Holland.

4. The Treaty of Nerchinsk established the Russo-Chinese border along the Amur River. Golovin was a man of unusual education, for he conducted the negotiations with the Portuguese Jesuit advisers of the Chinese emperor in Latin, dispensing with the Mongol intermediaries that the Russians and the Chinese had used before in dealings with each other.

5. Historians have traditionally cited Sokovnin's supposed adherence to Old Belief as one of the causes, based on A. A. Matveev's statement in his history of Peter that Sokovnin was a dissenter. The fully preserved documents of the investigation and trial make no mention of any religious issues, however, including Old Belief. Matveev and later historians were probably misled by the story of Sokovnin's sister, the Old Belief martyr "boiarynia Morozova" (died 1675), the subject of the famous painting by Vasili Surikov from 1887. Old Belief sources also make no mention of adherence to Old Belief by Morozova's brothers. Sokovnin may have been fearful of foreign cultures, but was not an Old Believer.

6. Tobacco was considered sinful by the Orthodox Church in the seventeenth century. Traditionally Russia had been more friendly to Protestants than Catholics, allowing German Lutherans to build a church in Moscow from the end of the sixteenth century. Foreign Calvinists eventually received the same permission, but the first Catholic priests in Moscow were allowed only in the 1680s. After their expulsion in 1689, Peter allowed them to return incognito in 1692 and openly from 1698. Adrian was not, however, a simple conservative: Opposed to foreign religions, tobacco, and the shaving of beards, he supported other Western-oriented cultural activities in education and literature.

7. This informality was not the result of imitating Europe, for Western court protocol was extremely formal. Peter disliked it intensely, especially the very stiff ceremonial of the Viennese court.

8. The exceptions were A. L. Ordin-Nashchokin (1667–72), Matveev (1672–76), V. S. Volynskii (1681–82), and Prince V. V. Golitsyn (1682–89). After 1689 Peter appointed Emel'ian Ukraintsev, again a Duma secretary, to the office, which he held until 1699.

9. Augustus wanted to capture Riga and Livonia from Sweden, while Denmark wanted the provinces lost in 1645–58.

10. A woman with uncovered hair was considered immodest in Russian tradition, an idea that persisted among the peasantry into the twentieth century. The low-cut dresses, by contrast, were less problematic. In 1707–8 several aristocratic women, including some of Peter's relatives, were denounced for wearing traditional garb when they could get away with it. Peter took no action on the denunciation.

Chapter Four

The Era of Experimentation, 1700–1716

When Peter's new army marched off to its first great battle and first defeat at Narva in 1700, Peter had devised a way to run his country by ignoring rather than displacing the traditional elite. Within a decade he realized that his tasks were too great for such an improvisation, and began to devise new structures to govern Russia. To staff these new structures he turned mainly to the sons of the traditional elite, the sons of the old boyars whose titles he had allowed to disappear but whose families remained at the pinnacle of society.

The improvised administrative structures of 1699–1708 did not entirely displace the old chancelleries. Most of them continued to exist, though many of them found their tasks taken over by the new ad hoc appointees. Peter did set up a Privy Chancellery to get the chancery heads together to coordinate policy, but it met rarely and concentrated on routine financial issues. Government rested to a large extent on a few men, at first primarily Fyodor Golovin, admiral, field marshal, and head of foreign policy. Many of the others were men of lesser rank, like Andrei Vinius or Aleksei Kurbatov, with whom Peter often corresponded directly. Vinius, for example was in charge not only of the procurement and supply of artillery, but also of many goods coming from Siberia. Golovin as well had many disparate duties, and various parts of the country were under his control.

The result was that Golovin was not only immensely powerful but also immensely overworked.

As field marshal, Golovin accompanied Peter to Narva. The capture of the Estonian port of Narva from Sweden was to be the first step in opening the window into Europe. Unfortunately for the Russians, King Charles XII of Sweden had knocked Denmark out of the war in a few weeks, and Augustus II was too slow in moving toward Riga. While Peter laid siege to Narva, Charles swiftly marched up and defeated the Russians in November 1700. Most of Peter's officers and many men were captured, and he had to start over with building his army, providing new recruits, horses, uniforms, ammunition, and transportation for the troops. They all had to be assembled on the northwestern frontier near Novgorod and Pskov, for Charles's army had camped immediately to the west in Swedish Livonia. Peter had no way of knowing where Charles would move next.

In 1701 Charles moved south into Poland, giving Peter a much-needed breathing space, which the tsar used to reequip his army. Peter appointed the aristocrat and boyar B. P. Sheremetev field marshal and put him in charge of the main armies harrying the Swedish possessions. In 1702 Peter moved against the Swedish forts in Ingria, the territory along the southern shore of the Gulf of Finland, which Sweden had wrested from Russia in 1609–18. In the fall of that year he took Nöteborg, near the beginning of the Neva River at Lake Ladoga. Nöteborg was just an improved version of the medieval Russian fort of Oreshek ("the Nut"), which Peter rebaptised with the German name Schlüsselburg ("Key Castle"). At the capture of Nöteborg, Alexander Menshikov, mainly Peter's personal friend until that moment, distinguished himself enough to cause Peter to promise him a reward: When the Russians captured the rest of Ingria, Menshikov would govern it.

That step came the next year. A small Russian force sailed down the Neva to capture the Swedish batteries at Nyenskans, a tiny settlement and fort a few miles from the place where the

Neva River flowed into the Baltic. Here Peter decided to build a fort and a new city, St. Petersburg, as a port for Russia on the Baltic. Like Oreshek, the area had been part of Russia before 1618, but had no major settlement or port for the swamps were too formidable. By 1703, however, the new methods for draining swamps pioneered by the Dutch had changed all that, and Peter knew all about these methods from his trip to Holland. Work began immediately, and as he had promised, Menshikov was in charge. He remained in charge of building and defending the new city for most of Peter's reign.

The rise of Menshikov added a new element to the mix at Peter's court. He and Golovin seem to have gotten along well enough, though Golovin was increasingly frustrated by the need to coordinate policy with Menshikov as well as Peter. Discontent among the aristocracy was quick to grow, and they began to criticize Menshikov for policies that were really Peter's idea. Hostile rumors abounded. Supposedly Menshikov had put a tax on wood, even on wooden coffins, and the proceeds were going into his own pocket, not that of the tsar. Even more serious, the belief among some was that Menshikov had bewitched the tsar, and then there was the rumor that the favorite had pulled Tsarevich Aleksei's hair and the tsar had done nothing. According to the Prussian Ambassador Johann Georg, Baron von Keyserling, when new taxes were being discussed:

> a very great lamentation has therefore arisen and because the favorite is entirely for the project since he will get a new rank, so the hatred against him becomes greater from day to day; all the great of this country are also very discontented and it is a matter of concern that if the King of Sweden with his army came right up to this border and gave a little air to the discontented, then probably a general revolt would follow.

There were other complaints that Menshikov had taken all fisheries under his control, even in the Ukraine. Indeed it was true that he administered many of the new taxes. In early 1704 Peter decreed a series of new minor taxes, on mills, bathhouses, and other items. The new duties all flowed into the Ingrian Chancellery. Running this office was Menshikov, and the revenue went to support the army and build the new city.

Menshikov's influence with the tsar went beyond friendship and administrative competence. In 1703 Peter's long-lasting liaison with Anna Mons came to an end, and in her place soon came a Lithuanian serving maid, Marta Skavronskaia, as she was known. Marta first came to Russia with her master, the German pastor Ernst Glück of Marienburg in Livonia, a noted educator and linguist. Much of her history is legend, but we have reliable evidence that she soon came to live in the household of Peter's sister Natalia. Marta was close friends with Menshikov's mistress and later wife, Daria Arseneva, herself the daughter of a noblewoman who had served in the household of Peter's mother. Marta replaced Anna in the tsar's affections about this time, cementing further Menshikov's influence as Anna had reflected and cemented that of Lefort in earlier years. Marta, soon to be christened Catherine in the Orthodox Church, was rapidly becoming a major figure at court.

The most serious of the rivalries among the elite in these years was that between Menshikov and field marshal Sheremetev. The governance of Ingria gave the favorite important military commands, taking authority and troops from Sheremetev. Keyserling reported:

> Two weeks ago the Field marshal Sheremetev left from here completely discontented, since the favorite Aleksander Danilovich at his own pleasure not only sought out the best and most experienced officers from his [Sheremetev's] whole army and engaged them with his regiment, but also recently remain under his command the whole time in Ingria, about which the Field marshal himself, who tried to oppose the order brought by his majesty the tsar in person with some representations, had to swallow some very hard words.

In 1705 the musketeers and townsmen of Astrakhan' rose in rebellion, mainly against exploitation and arbitrary behavior by their superiors, but also in favor of beards and the old ways. Peter sent Sheremetev away from the army to suppress the revolt and wild rumors flew about Moscow: Sheremetev wanted to spare the rebels, but Peter wanted harsh repression (the opposite was true). Sheremetev would make a deal with the rebels. He would join the rebels to his army and overthrow Menshikov. None of this came to pass, and the field marshal took the town by storm, smashing the rebellion, but the rumors revealed the scale of discontent and his personal popularity.

The new Danish envoy, Georg Grund, believed that Peter could succeed at his reforms if he had time enough, but the problem was that everything rested on him. If he fell ill or died, all the reforms and the war would come to an end. Unfortunately this would probably mean the end of the throne for the heir Aleksei Petrovich, since he "was not so brought up that his subjects have any respect for him." The universal favorite was Sheremetev, "of whose great qualities all Russia was persuaded," especially the earlier boyar opponents of the throne. They also liked Sheremetev "because he is a great general and his father and grandfather were already their commanders, and thus he is in all respects the most distinguished among them."

The rivalries in the army eventually came to a resolution by the end of 1706. That summer Golovin suddenly died, leaving Menshikov in undisputed possession of Peter's favor. The role of principal coordinator now passed to Menshikov, assisted by lesser officials. In the army, after a brief flirtation with an attempt to put a Scottish-Austrian professional soldier, Georg von Ogilvy, at the head, Peter appointed Sheremetev the first field marshal. The tsar was not afraid of Sheremetev's popularity. Peter put Menshikov in charge of the cavalry, which lessened the area of potential conflicts between the field marshal and the favorite. The resolution of the army rivalries had considerable impact on the civilian government, for Menshikov played a major role in both. It meant the continuation of the policy of centralization of government around Peter and the favorite, substituting Menshikov for Golovin.

The compromise in the army came none too soon, for at the end of 1706 Charles XII managed to defeat Augustus II of Saxony and Poland and eject him from the throne of Poland. Augustus was compelled to sign a humiliating peace, and Charles placed a Swedish puppet, the Polish magnate Stanislaw Leszczynski (1677–1766), on the Polish throne. Peter now had no allies, and in the summer of 1708 Charles moved his army east through Poland toward the Russian border. Precisely at this time Peter abandoned the attempt to run his government through ad hoc arrangements around Menshikov and a few other trusted counselors. In their place he divided the country up into nine large provinces, or *gubernias*. In each *gubernia* the governor had complete control over tax collection, disbursements for local needs, appointment of his subordinates, and justice. He had only to turn over the very large sums needed for the army and in all respects was answerable only to the tsar. Peter did not appoint favorites to the new positions, only Menshikov was in that category, and Menshikov's only ally among the governors was his client Gagarin. Indeed most of the *gubernias* went to the aristocracy. In the first year of the new system, 1709, these powerful new governors were

Petersburg—Prince A. D. Menshikov
Archangel—Prince P. A. Golitsyn
Moscow—Tikhon Streshnev
Smolensk—P. S. Saltykov
Kazan'—P. M. Apraksin
Kiev—Prince D. M. Golitsyn
Voronezh—F. M. Apraksin
Azov—I. A. Tolstoi
Siberia—Prince M. P. Gagarin

Of these nine men, only Menshikov, his client Prince Gagarin, and I. A. Tolstoi were not scions of highly aristocratic families, though Gagarin and Tolstoi were certainly noblemen.[1] Tolstoi's brother Petr was already an important diplomat serving in Istanbul and would later on rise to greater heights. The two Princes Golitsyn were great aristocrats and the Apraksins and Saltykov were both relatives of Peter's by the marriage of their sisters to his half-brothers Fyodor and Ivan. As the tsar's relatives, they too were now aristocrats. Streshnev was a relative of Peter's childhood tutor and thus also related to the tsar through Peter's grandmother. The two Princes Golitsyn and Saltykov stand out by the importance of their duties in governing the crucial border areas. Kiev was the main center of Russian power in the Ukraine, facing Crimea and the Ottomans as well as Poland, and Smolensk was the key fortress and principal city on the road west from Moscow. Any invader coming from Poland had to first take Smolensk. Archangel was the center of Russia's foreign trade. Though these aristocratic governors controlled strategic border areas and huge territories, they were not chosen for their experience. Only Menshikov and Streshnev had served in high positions before (Streshnev as head of the Military Chancellery, the *Razriad*). Later developments would show that some new appointees were not even Peter's loyal supporters in the elite, for both Petr Apraksin and Prince D. M. Golitsyn at different times would oppose Peter and his legacy. For the time being, however, they held the power at home while Peter followed the army as Charles seemed to be moving relentlessly east toward Moscow. Charles was fully aware of the discontent among the Russian elite as well as the people and intended to exploit it, to put the aristocrats in power in place of Peter and perhaps even to break up the country into separate principalities. Sweden had no desire for a modern, vigorous Russia on its eastern frontier.

To accomplish these aims Charles had first to get to Moscow. All through 1708 his army moved east. Peter resolved not to give battle until the Swedish army reached his frontier where he could replenish his army easily in case of defeat. He did not fear the discontented nobles who figured so largely in Charles's plans. At first Charles was successful: In July 1708, he defeated Prince Repnin at Golovchino in eastern Poland and moved on, through trackless forests and villages stripped of their provisions by the retreating Russians. Skirmishes were continual, and officers in the Swedish army began to note with alarm that the Russians, particularly the junior officers so long a problem to Peter, were learning how to fight. Scottish Captain James Jeffreyes, a volunteer with Charles XII's army, reported,

> The Swedes now own the Muscovites have learnt their lesson much better than they had either at the battles of Narva or Fraustadt, and that they equal if not exceed the Saxons both in discipline and valor, 'tis true their cavalry is not able to cope with owrs, but their infantry stand their ground obstinately.

The Swedish army began to run out of food and ammunition, and Charles ordered General Löwenhaupt to march southeast from Riga to join him with the supply train and fresh troops. Meanwhile the Swedish king got up to the Russian border and waited. Perhaps he was waiting for news of a revolt, but it did not come. After a few days, he decided to turn south, toward the Ukraine, where a softer climate meant more abundant supplies, at least in theory.

Peter learned of the approach of the Swedish reinforcements, and struck swiftly at Lesnaia (September 28/October 8, 1708), cutting off the supply train while Löwenhaupt escaped to join his king, bringing fresh troops but also new mouths to feed. Charles moved on south, where the only aristocratic discontent to emerge during the campaign appeared with the decision of Ukrainian Hetman Ivan Mazepa and some of his Cossack officers to go over to Sweden. With a few thousand Cossacks they joined the Swedish king at the border. Charles had expected the entire Cossack army, but it did not materialize. The Cossack rank and file remained loyal to Peter, who sent Menshikov to smash the center of resistance at Baturin and see to the election of a new hetman, Ivan Skoropads'kyi, in place of Mazepa. Peter had checked Charles's move.

With the Swedes in winter quarters in the Ukraine, Peter moved his main army south to watch and harry them. When spring came, Charles began to move northeast again, but he first wanted to take the fortified towns in the area. His army lay siege to the small Ukrainian town of Poltava in May, and now Peter decided to give battle. He marched his army to within a few miles north of the town and waited for Charles to attack, which the Swedish king did on June 27 (July 8), 1709. By noon it was all over, Sweden had gone down to utter defeat, and the Russians captured the whole Swedish army save Charles himself and his personal guards, who fled to Turkey. The news stunned Europe and created a new international system overnight. Russia was now a major power. Peter hastened to rebuild his alliances with Denmark and Saxony-Poland, and in the next year he captured the remaining Swedish towns in Livonia and Estonia (Riga and Reval) as well as Viborg in southeastern Finland. He thus secured the approaches to his new capital as well as taking three important commercial ports. His window to the West was safe.

REFORM AT HOME

The radical change in the military and international position of Russia allowed Peter to turn to domestic affairs, and over the next few years he rebuilt both the formal and informal structures of power in Russia. During the 1708–9 campaign a new favorite emerged as a rival to Menshikov, Prince Vasilii Vladimirovich Dolgorukii, who belonged to one of the most aristocratic clans in the country. At the Poltava victory parade in Moscow Menshikov rode on one side of the tsar and on the other Dolgorukii, who had also received the command of the Preobrazhenskii guards on the eve of the battle. Early in 1711, Peter also announced that he would marry his mistress Marta, the now Orthodox Catherine. This would regularize his private life, legitimize his daughters by Catherine, and create a whole new grouping at court.

Perhaps the first sign that Peter wanted to rebuild the formal structure of power as well came in 1710, when the diplomatic corps noticed that Peter suddenly invited them to formal audiences in the rarely used Kremlin palace, audiences put on with full magnificence, albeit in a more European than traditional Russian style. The days of camping out with the army and the modest house in Preobrazhenskoe seemed to be over. More fundamental was Peter's decision to grant to the newly conquered Baltic provinces, Estonia and Livonia, their traditional rights of self-government, both for the towns and the German nobility of the countryside. In both provinces a Russian governor presided over a local government whose privileges were even greater than those under the last kings of Sweden. The Baltic nobles began to arrive at the new court in St. Petersburg, forming a new and crucial element in the Russian elite that retained its importance until 1917.

Even more important was the establishment of the Senate in 1711, at first a temporary measure devised to manage affairs during the short-lived Prut campaign against the Turks.[2] The Senate was to coordinate policy over the eight "big" *gubernias*, collect and disburse the taxes the governors collected, act as the court of appeals, and supervise lower-level appointments. It also had special agents to investigate corruption, the *fiskaly*, for Peter was becoming aware of the scale of malfeasance among his officials.

The senators appointed in 1711 were not a very distinguished lot: Prince V. V. Dolgorukii's brother Mikhail was the most aristocratic, and besides him the clan had a client in Grigorii Plemiannikov, a naval official. Field Marshal Sheremetev had two clients among the senators, one M. M. Samarin, a former army paymaster, and V. A. Apukhtin, who had held a similar position. Prince Grigorii Volkonskii seems to have been Menshikov's client. Senator Tikhon Streshnev and Prince Petr Golitsyn had both been governors of the new *gubernias*, were both aristocrats, and were nobody's client. Similarly Senator Ivan Musin-Pushkin was a relative of Patriarch Ioakim, a highly educated man who spoke Latin to foreign dignitaries and had been a major figure in court and government for decades. He headed the Monastery Chancellery, which collected revenue from the vast church landholdings to fill Peter's treasury, giving the monasteries only a small grant. As in the case of the appointments to the governorships in 1708–9, Menshikov did not do very well, for he had only his client Volkonskii among aristocrats and their clients.

The character of the Senate changed rapidly as some of the less aristocratic senators dropped out of the picture and as the Senate acquired a new and vigorous president almost immediately and largely through sheer accident. Prince Iakov Fyodorovich Dolgorukii had been a prisoner of war in Sweden since the defeat at Narva in 1700. In the spring of 1711, as Sweden's position grew more and more critical, the government decided to send Dolgorukii and a group of other Russian prisoners from the comparative comfort of Stockholm to the far north of Sweden. They put them on a ship headed up the Gulf of Bothnia, but on the way Dolgorukii and his companions seized control and forced the captain to take them back to Russia. The Swedish captain told the Russians that he could not, since he did not know the waters, so Prince Iakov (as he later wrote Peter) put his faith in Saint Nicholas, the patron saint of sailors, and landed safely on the coast of Estonia, Russia's new conquest. When Peter heard of the bold escape, he was overjoyed and immediately appointed Dolgorukii to the presidency of the Senate. Dolgorukii was the eldest of his clan, a man who had already been on an embassy to France in 1684–86 and served Peter from the beginning of the reign. His appointment also meant that the new favorite, Prince V. V. Dolgorukii, had his brother Mikhail, his client Plemiannikov, and in Prince Iakov the eldest and most authoritative member of the whole clan in the Senate. Once again, Menshikov's overwhelming power had been diminished by the establishment of new institutions in which he had a role but could not dominate. To be sure, he remained the governor of Ingria, responsible for its defense and administration, and for the building of the new city of St. Petersburg. Since Peter began to move the government to St. Petersburg in 1712–13, this was hardly a minor responsibility, but the new instruments of the central government were in the hands of the old aristocracy and their clients, not of Menshikov.

As we shall see, there was more to the rivalry of Menshikov and the Dolgorukiis than just personalities. The Dolgorukiis and their allies came more and more to oppose Peter's policies, though they were happy to use the new forms of government. Neither the Dolgorukiis nor the other aristocratic senators, however, were pious old boyars yearning for the days of undisturbed Orthodox piety and ignorant of European culture. Just as Sheremetev was so fascinated with Catholicism that he almost converted, Dolgorukii was also no friend to narrow Orthodoxy. The affair of Grigorii Tveritinov, trivial in itself, shows his views very clearly.

Tveritinov was a surgeon in Moscow, then a profession in Europe as well as Russia akin to barbering. Nevertheless, it required some elementary education, and he seems to have even learned Latin and perhaps German. Tveritinov began to read books about religion borrowed from friends and talk about it with his foreign colleagues. He began to doubt the Orthodox reverence for icons and to elaborate a semi-Protestant doctrine of his own. In 1713 someone denounced him for heterodox views and after he was interrogated under torture, he fled to St. Petersburg. There he placed himself under the protection of the Senate, and particularly of Iakov Dolgorukii. The de facto head of the church, Stefan Iavorskii, was outraged and implacable, demanding the execution of Tveritinov and his associates. The senators, however, would not give in, and after a special trial (with Menshikov, Streshnev, Musin-Pushkin, and the governor of Kiev, Prince D. M. Golitsyn), Stefan failed to secure a conviction. Finally Peter ordered the case closed early in 1716, and Tveritinov had to confess his errors and remain under the watch of his bishop. One unrepentant follower was executed. Stefan, who had held out for maximum punishment, lost, and as much because of the Senate as because of Peter.[3]

The aristocratic Senators were not willing to execute Tveritinov just to please the church. If Menshikov and the Senators did not have radically different views on cultural and religious issues, the rivalry was no less real. It came to the surface when Menshikov made a series of mistakes that temporarily cost him the tsar's trust. The first mistake came out of the tangled politics connected with the continuing war with Sweden. After Sweden's defeats at Peter's hands Charles XII was stuck in the Ottoman Empire, far from his country. Its possessions in northern Germany (Bremen, Stralsund, Stettin, and other places), acquired sixty years before in the Thirty Years' War, were exposed to its envious neighbors. Not only Denmark and Saxony-Poland were interested in the Swedish holdings, but also Hanover and Prussia. As Peter could not guarantee the continued possession of St. Petersburg and other conquests, he had to go on fighting to force Charles XII to surrender on his terms. In other words, he had to help his allies take Sweden's German possessions. In 1713 Peter put Menshikov in charge of a Russian army, which would cooperate with Denmark and other powers to wrest these small but valuable territories from Sweden.

Menshikov quickly got into trouble with Peter when the remaining Swedish field army surrendered to the allies in Holstein. Peter insisted that Russia get most of the prisoners, since Russia had done more of the fighting, and he wanted to use the prisoners to force Charles to exchange them for the Russians captured at Narva. Menshikov failed to do that, and rumors immediately reached Peter that Menshikov had been bribed. This was bad enough, but later in the year Menshikov's army with some Prussian help took the town of Stettin from Sweden. He handed it over to Prussia, which Peter approved, but with conditions that Peter did not approve. The tsar was furious and ordered his diplomats to rewrite the agreement with Berlin.[4] Issues trivial in themselves had badly damaged Menshikov's credit with his master the tsar.

There matters stood for several months. Peter's army captured Finland from Sweden in 1713–14, giving the tsar a large bargaining chip in future peace negotiations and totally isolating Sweden. His conquest was sealed with the small but crucial naval victory over Sweden at the battle of the Hangö peninsula on July 27, 1714. A few months later Charles XII managed to get out of Turkey to try to restore order in his kingdom, making Peter and his allies fear that more serious fighting might be ahead.

For the time being, however, Peter could return to St. Petersburg and celebrate his naval victory. Soon afterward he turned to a wholly new matter, the massive corruption that he had uncovered on the part of Menshikov and other officials. After Menshikov's name day celebration on November 23, 1714, Peter turned to Menshikov to tell him what he had discovered. Danish envoy Peter Falck reported the gist of Peter's tirade, which lasted for two hours:

> Well Alexander! Today I saw the marks of your faithlessness. I raised you up from nothing but you are raising yourself above me; I knew well that you were robbing me and I permitted it, but now I am well informed that you have not only stolen hundreds of thousands but millions and just this year you have stolen more than a million. Prince Menshikov wanted to excuse himself and said, among other things, that he saw well that after the complaints which Your Majesty [the King of Denmark] made against him, the tsar no longer loved him. The tsar responded that he had no more

excuse and that he knew very well what he had done in Holstein and that he had not yet pardoned him for it. The tsaritsa wanted to interpose herself, but the tsar told her, "Madame, this is not your business. I am not angry but I speak the truth and this is in earnest." Prince Menshikov seeing no other help began to weep and begged his tsarish majesty to take everything, adding these words, "father, everything is yours."

The tsar then launched a massive investigation into the charges, and to Menshikov's horror he learned that his chief rival, Prince V. V. Dolgorukii, headed the investigation. The commission arrested dozens of officials, many of them Menshikov's assistants (the vice governor of Ingria Iakov Rimskii-Korsakov) or his clients, Prince G. I. Volkonskii, Prince M. P. Gagarin (the governor of Siberia), and an admiralty official until then close to both Menshikov and the tsar, Alexander Kikin. Kikin's was a name Peter would come to loathe in future years.

Menshikov's machinations were exposed to view. He had made enormous sums by overcharging the treasury for goods to be supplied to the army and toward the construction of St. Petersburg. He had manipulated grain prices and the prices of imported luxury goods through his business agent in Amsterdam. He had spent the state treasury's money on himself and concealed the expenditure. Ultimately the favorite was condemned to pay a gigantic fine, over a million rubles, so as to return his ill-gotten gains to the treasury.[5] He had to dissolve his personal guards and military regiments, and lost some other privileges, but he retained his offices and his rank. His associates in crime, Rimskii-Korsakov and the Senator Prince Volkonskii, as well as Senator Apukhtin, who managed corruption on his own, were whipped, had their nostrils slit, and were exiled to Siberia. Kikin, however, got off lightly: he suffered no corporal punishment and was exiled first to Kazan' and then to Moscow. He was back in Petersburg by the summer of 1715. Apparently it was Peter's wife Catherine who had interceded for both Menshikov and

Kikin. In the case of Kikin, it was a decision she would come to regret, for Kikin was filled with rage in spite of his escape from punishment.

Thus by 1715 Menshikov seemed to have fallen from the position of one of the two chief favorites of the tsar to that of a moderately important government official. Then fate intervened on his behalf in two ways, by the birth of two heirs to the throne in autumn 1715, and the next year by the Senate's mistakes in managing the war. The Senate's mistake, if that is what it was, came when Peter was in Denmark trying to arrange a joint Russian–Danish landing on the southern coast of Sweden.[6] Peter finally decided to cancel the expedition, but a diversionary operation in Finland was already under way. It was the simultaneous diversion in Finland that the Senate bungled.

The plan had been to send an army corps and the galley fleet to southwestern Finland to raid Sweden and make a small landing to draw off Swedish troops from the south. However, when the Russian army under Prince M. M. Golitsyn reached the jumping-off point its food supplies began to run low. Golitsyn sent messenger after messenger to St. Petersburg asking for supplies, but the Senate, responsible for such matters in the tsar's absence, did nothing. Golitsyn's letters to Peter produced urgent requests to the Senate, but the result was only a shouting match with Menshikov. By August disease and hunger were decimating the Russian army and Menshikov decided to take charge. He ordered all ships in the port of St. Petersburg seized, confiscated all food supplies he could find, and shipped them off to Golitsyn just in time to avert disaster. Menshikov then informed Peter of the events. Menshikov was back in the tsar's good graces and in planning next year's campaign Peter wrote to the senators, "This time it is you who will answer." However much Dolgorukii might discover that Menshikov had stolen, Peter would forgive (and fine) him, but the senators were out of his good graces forever.

ALEKSEI PETROVICH

The other turn of fate that would help Menshikov to return to un-challenged influence with Peter occurred in the autumn of 1715. Almost on the same day Peter's wife Catherine bore him a son, named Petr Petrovich, and Aleksei's wife, Charlotte, gave birth to another boy, baptized Petr Alekseevich, Peter's grandson. Every-one assumed that Tsarevich Aleksei was the heir to the Russian throne, but the birth of Petr Petrovich brought into existence a potential rival. In Europe the succession would have been clear, following the male line, so that Aleksei's son would inherit no matter how many other sons Peter might produce. Indeed the usual situation in Russia had been the same, that the eldest son succeeded his father on the throne, but there was no formal law requiring this. Furthermore Russian inheritance customs, unlike European, did not require the exclusion of younger brothers. Rus-sia even had a precedent where the throne had gone to a second son rather than to a grandson by the presumed heir.[7] Thus the throne now had, in theory, two possible heirs, Aleksei and Peter's new son, Petr Petrovich. Catherine, and thus her ally Menshikov, would obviously benefit from the second solution.

The birth of the two boys would not have made much differ-ence if Peter's relations with his eldest son, Tsarevich Aleksei, had not been deteriorating for years. At the time of Peter's di-vorce from Evdokiia in 1698 the boy had been taken from his mother's side, and when the divorce was complete, Peter gave Aleksei over to the care of his sister Natalia and Menshikov. This was a serious break with tradition, since the tutor of the tsar's sons had always been a great nobleman, often a relative. The tradition was also to give the sons teachers who were experts (of-ten learned monks) to teach them reading, writing, and the other necessary subjects. Peter and Menshikov looked abroad for such teachers, finally settling on a German baron, Heinrich Huyssen. Under the baron's tutelage Aleksei acquired a Western education.

He learned German, some Polish, Latin, and French, and he was exposed to the secular knowledge that young European noblemen and princes received at that time. His education may not have been brilliant, but he mastered some history, geography, military sciences, and arithmetic, as well as moral instruction adapted to the needs of future rulers. By 1707, when Aleksei was seventeen, Peter put him in charge of the defenses of Moscow, ordering him to modernize the fortifications and make sure the troops were ready for combat if Charles XII were to get that far and the need arise. Aleksei remained at that post until after Poltava.

With the victory over Sweden Peter had suddenly become very important in Europe and simultaneously he decided that it was time for his son to be married. He began to explore possible brides among the European princely houses and by 1710 he found one, Charlotte, the daughter of the Duke of Braunschweig-Wolfenbüttel. This was a minor German duchy, but well connected: Charlotte's sister was married to the Holy Roman Emperor Karl VI, reigning in Vienna. Peter ordered Aleksei to join him in Germany, and the tsarevich came to Dresden, the fashionable capital of Saxony. There he enjoyed himself under the guidance of Charlotte's relatives, going to the French comedies at the court theater and flirting with aristocratic ladies. In the fall of 1711 Aleksei was married in Torgau, in the palace chapel of the dowager electress of Saxony.

Aleksei and his new wife did not move on to St. Petersburg immediately. Peter continued to require his son to work to supply the army, much of which was quartered then in Poland. Aleksei spent nearly a year in Torun, in northern Poland, gradually running out of money and spending more and more time away from Charlotte. On their arrival in the new Russian capital in 1713, there was much ceremony but Charlotte did not feel much at home. Only Peter himself was really kind to her, and she could see that Catherine and Menshikov saw Aleksei as a rival and tried to make trouble for the young couple. The favorite told Aleksei that Charlotte was arrogant and did not love him, and that her attitude was not surprising given how the tsarevich treated his wife. She reported in a letter to her mother that he told her that he did not care about her at all, to which she replied that no shoemaker or tailor in Germany would treat his wife the way Aleksei treated her. His reply was, "You are not in Germany, you are here." Aleksei ignored her more and more openly. Habsburg Ambassador Pleyer reported in August 1713, that he had learned that "the tsarevich had brought little German inclination and customs back from Germany and passed most of his time with Muscovite priests and bad common fellows, and at the same time was strongly given to drink."

The presence of Aleksei's many friends in the church has often been taken to show that he was a religious conservative, longing for the return of Old Muscovite piety and ways. In fact Aleksei was closer to Sheremetev or Metropolitan Stefan Iavorskii in his religious views; that is, he read works of Catholic piety and was intensely interested in non-Orthodox confessions, but remained loyal to Orthodoxy in the end. He corresponded and exchanged religious books with Ukrainian clergy in Kiev and with Prince D. M. Golitsyn, the governor of Kiev who was good friends with many local monks and priests. Early on Stefan Iavorskii himself thought of Aleksei as an alternative to Peter. Stefan was particularly incensed that the newly established *fiskaly* be turned over to the treasury and on March 17, 1712, he preached a sermon about them. Stefan attacked the *fiskaly* as irresponsible slanderers, but also raised touchier matters. He attacked those who put away their wives and did not observe all the Orthodox fasts, a group that included the tsar himself. At the end he called on Saint Alexius, whose feast day it was, not to forget his namesake, the tsarevich: "You left your house, he also wanders among alien houses; you left your parents, he also; you were deprived of slaves, servants, subjects, friends, relatives, acquaintances, he also; you are a man of God, he is also and a true servant of Christ. Let us pray, saint of God, protect your namesake, our only hope." Stefan offended even the Senate, for the next day the senators present came to him to complain that he was encouraging rebellion and touched the tsar's honor, to say nothing of the question of the *fiskaly*. The metropolitan begged Peter's forgiveness, claiming rather disingenuously that he had intended no specific reference. Aleksei had become the hope of the church, not to return ancient piety but simply to defend its position, financial and otherwise, against the reforming tsar. He had also become the enemy of Menshikov and his ally Catherine.

Peter made one last effort in 1714 to use his son to help him in government but nothing much came of it. During the eclipse of Menshikov we hear very little of Aleksei, who was also ill much of the time. The relationship of father and son, political as well as personal, exploded on the birth of the two potential heirs at the end of 1715. The problem that immediately arose was that Peter made it clear that he regarded his new son, Petr Petrovich, as his heir, not Aleksei or Aleksei's son Petr Alekseevich, the tsar's grandson. To complicate matters further, the unhappy Charlotte died in childbirth. Unless he remarried, Aleksei would have no more potential heirs.

At one of the celebrations for the birth of his son Peter had a long talk with Danish Ambassador Hans Georg von Westphalen about the regency after the death of Louis XIV of France, who had died only two months before. The tsar brought up the subject and told Westphalen that Louis XIV was clearly the greatest king France ever had and that he had admired his great and heroic actions. He could not, however, admire the arrangements he had made for his succession, the regency of the Duke of Orleans over the king's great-grandson, the young Louis XV. If Louis XIV had uncovered evidence of a future capability to rule in his great-grandson, he should not put him in the hands of a man who could easily poison the boy and take the throne for himself. If the duke was himself worthy to be king and Louis XV as unworthy as was being reported, Louis XIV should have just proclaimed Orleans the successor. Westphalen replied that the French fundamental laws obliged Louis to put the regency into the hands of the closest princes of the blood until his heir grew to maturity. The king of France could not just name anyone king; the act would be null and void, and besides could lead to civil war. The Dane's answer set off a tirade from Peter, one that explains more even than his letters to his son about what his thoughts were on the future in autumn 1715:

> Well, replied the tsar, then a prince who, to make for himself a state that is prosperous and redoubtable, has exposed his life a hundred times, sacrificed his health and brought by care and by skill his affairs to a conclusion by his application, and who has brought them to such a point as to make himself and his state respected and feared by all his neighbors, would pass the fruits of his labors into the hands of a fool so that the fool would begin the destruction of them.
>
> In truth I am not of your sentiments. It is not, it seems to me, right that a monarch only strains himself to enlarge his states, makes them prosperous and makes himself feared during his lifetime, it is also necessary that he knows how to preserve his work after his death as well, which he will be able to do to best effect in taking great care to have a successor who is capable not only of preserving his acquisitions and establishments but of executing as well the rest of his plans. And if he has to choose one from among his subjects? You, he continued, do you tax him with cruelty, if a prince, to save and to preserve his state, which should be more precious than all the blood in his veins, would contrive to alter the succession of blood? And me, I would call it committing the greatest of cruelties to immolate the safety of the state simply to the established law of succession.

The succession had become an acute issue in Peter's mind, and he had no doubt that Aleksei opposed virtually everything he had accomplished.

Peter showed little interest in the birth of his grandson, but enormous joy at the birth of his son. He ordered vast celebrations with fireworks and free beer and vodka. The whole city and court got drunk. Menshikov drank so much he lost one of the jewel-encrusted medals Peter had given him and did not notice the loss until a soldier, who had found it in the street, brought it to him. Unfortunately Aleksei's son was visibly very healthy, while Peter's new son was extremely sickly and likely not to live very long.

Shortly after the ceremonies of baptism were over, Peter wrote to Aleksei. The letter chastised him for his inattention to military affairs and general unfitness to rule and threatened to disinherit him in Peter's will. Aleksei answered his father on October 31, agreeing that he was too lacking in intelligence and physical strength to rule, too "rotten." He asked his father to remove him from the succession in favor of his newborn brother, Petr Petrovich. Tsar Peter, who was ill at the time, replied to his son only on January 19, 1716:

Last reminder.

Since I could not give a resolution because of my illness, now I answer: I read your letter answering my first letter, in which you only mention the succession and put up to me everything which is always mine. And why did you not give an answer, as in my letter? For there I wrote much more about your lack of will and desire for affairs than about bodily weakness, which you alone mention. Also, you neglect and ignore the fact that I have been dissatisfied with you for years, even though I wrote a lot about that. For this reason I think you do not pay much attention to your father's order. Which moved me to write this last: for if you do not fear me now, how will you keep my testament after me? That you will swear an oath is impossible to believe because of your hardness of heart. Besides that there is the word of David: every man is a lie [Psalm 116, 11 = 115, 2]. Also, even if you truly wanted to keep it, the big beards,[8] who are not in influence now because of their idleness, and to whom you are now very inclined, will be able to incline you and force you.

And besides, with what will you return to your father for your birth? Will you help in my unbearable griefs and labors, when you acquire the same mature age? No, not at all! What is known to all is that you rather hate my tasks which I perform for my people without sparing my health, and finally you will be the destroyer of them. For this reason it is impossible for you to remain as you are, neither fish nor flesh; but either change your ways and sincerely make yourself worthy to be the heir, or be a monk; for without this my spirit cannot be quiet and especially now that I am not very healthy. To this give immediately your decision when you receive it, either in writing or by speaking to me. And if you don't do that, I will treat you like a malefactor.

Aleksei answered the next day in a letter of only a few lines that he chose to become a monk. Peter gave him time to think it over.

Aleksei took a long time to think it over. He said nothing for months, and unknown to Peter, he was talking to Alexander Kikin, the admiralty official convicted for corruption in 1714, and other malcontents about his plight. Some suggested that he give in and go to a monastery or accept his father's reproaches and wait for future events. Others suggested a more active path, and reminded him of the story of the False Dmitrii during the Time of Troubles and the attempts of the Stuarts to recover the throne of England with French help.[9]

Meanwhile, Peter pursued his plans in the war, went to Denmark for the abortive invasion, and restored Menshikov to favor after the Senate had botched the diversion plan in the summer. Then he summoned Aleksei to join him in Europe, for the tsar planned another journey to Holland and this time to go on to France. Though the summons obviously implied that Aleksei, if he behaved properly, would not be sent to a monastery and might be the heir as before, the tsarevich disobeyed. Perhaps he feared for his future with his archenemy Menshikov back in favor. In any case, on September 26, 1716, he told Menshikov that he was going to join his father in Germany and left St. Petersburg. As he took his farewell of the Senate, he whispered to Prince Iakov Dolgorukii, "Don't abandon me."

Aleksei did not go to join his father. Accompanied only by his mistress Evfrosinia and a few servants, he went to Vienna, to his brother-in-law by marriage, Karl VI, Holy Roman Emperor, to ask for help against Peter. The dissensions at the Russian court were out in the open.

It was eighteen years since Peter had returned from Europe the first time and concluded that he could not rely on either his relatives or other boyars to run the country properly and loyally. For a decade after that moment he had managed business with his favorites, Golovin and then Menshikov, as well as with lesser administrators like Vinius or Kurbatov. He wrote directly to all of these men, bypassing the chancelleries with their boyar heads. He ceased to appoint men to the Duma ranks and to call the Boyar Duma. He made the major decisions, treaties, wars, cultural changes, and the new taxes and administrative structure to support the war—and to build St. Petersburg—without consulting anyone but Golovin or Menshikov.

If Peter thought such a policy would work in the long run, he was wrong. In one important respect he came to realize early that he had to work with the aristocrats, in that he appointed Sheremetev to supreme command in the army. Sheremetev survived the attempt to appoint Ogilvy at his side as well as Menshikov's increasingly large military role, even though Sheremetev was early on the hope of the discontented in the nobility and the army.

Peter came to match his policy of reincorporating the aristocracy into the army with a similar policy in civilian affairs only with the establishment of the nine "big" *gubernias* in 1708. Here nine men, six of them great aristocrats, divided up the whole country among themselves with almost complete control of their districts. Only Peter himself stood above. This arrangement as well proved clumsy: Russia really had no central government and the tsar alone was not enough for coordination. The Senate, which began simply as a committee to govern Russia in the tsar's absence, turned into the central institution of the state. Peter's correspondence from that moment on is mainly with the Senate and the governors, not with the lesser officials as before. The Senate began as a body of aristocrats and their clients and became more aristocratic as time went on. Dominant in the Senate as at court were the Princes Dolgorukii, propelled into such power by the tsar's favor for Prince V. V. Dolgorukii from 1710 on and the eclipse of Menshikov in 1713–16.

The dominance of the Dolgorukiis and their allies was not merely the alternation of one group for another. The Dolgorukiis were closely allied with Tsarevich Aleksei, whose opposition to his father implied explicit opposition to most of Peter's reforms and achievements (if not the religious traditionalism of legend). This meant that the senatorial opposition and the tsarevich had become a danger for Peter personally but also for the changes that he had wrought in Russia. Peter would discover the extent and character of elite opposition only later, but for the moment the disappearance of his son into Austria was in itself a cause for grave concern.

NOTES

1. Princely titles in Russia did not necessarily imply aristocratic status. Since all sons and daughters of a prince inherited the title, after several generations in each princely line there were many descendants with a title but without wealth or position.

2. In 1711 the Ottoman Turks, encouraged by Sweden's ally France, declared war on Russia. Peter's army advanced along the Prut River into

Ottoman-held Moldavia and was quickly surrounded. The Russians negotiated a truce with the Turks (many of whose leaders were unenthusiastic
about the war), surrendering Azov in the process and reducing the number
of new *gubernias* from nine to eight. Peter was able to extricate himself
and the army by August 1711, though the negotiations for a final peace
dragged on for years.

3. Stefan's only solace was to compose a massive tract (*Kamen'
very*, "*The Rock of Faith*") to attack Tveritinov and Protestantism and
defend the authority of the church and clergy. Peter refused to let it
be printed.

4. The Duke of Holstein had inserted himself into the surrender negotiations. Prussia desperately wanted the town for commercial reasons
and made a deal with Holstein and Menshikov that gave the town jointly
to Prussia and Holstein and incidentally also committed Russia to help
Prussia support Holstein claims against Denmark, Peter's ally. Peter had
no objection to Prussia taking Stettin, but he would not hear of supporting Holstein against his Danish ally and negotiated a new agreement
with Prussia without that clause.

5. To put the sum in perspective, Russia's entire budget in 1709 con-
sisted of some three and a half million rubles in income and a bit more
in expenditures, rising to seven million by 1720.

6. The landing would allow Denmark to recover the provinces lost
in 1658 and hopefully force Charles XII to make peace. Peter's generals on the spot and Menshikov from St. Petersburg advised against it,
arguing that the Swedish army was still formidable and that the Danes
were unreliable.

7. Vasilii III, who succeeded Ivan III in 1505, was the second son
of his father by a second marriage and displaced Dmitrii, the son of the
eldest son of Ivan by his first wife.

8. The "big beards" refers to the clergy, who were allowed to retain
their beards when Peter ordered the boyars and nobles to shave in 1698.

9. The Glorious Revolution of 1688 overthrew King James II of England and Scotland. He and his son, James Stuart, made repeated attempts
to land in Scotland or Ireland with French troops to recover their throne.
The first such attempt to have momentary success took place in Scotland
in 1715, the last in 1745 under James Stuart's son Charles.

FURTHER READING

Bushkovitch, Paul. *Peter the Great: The Struggle for Power 1671–1725.* Cambridge, UK: Cambridge University Press, 2001.

——. "Poltava's Consequences: Local Autonomy in the Russian Empire in the Reign of Peter the Great," in Serhii Plokhy ed., *Poltava 1709: The Battle and the Myth* (*Harvard Ukrainian Studies*) 31, nos. 1–4 (2009–10): 135–58.

Englund, Peter. *The Battle of Poltava: The Birth of the Russian Empire.* London: Gollancz, 1992.

LeDonne, John P. *Absolutism and Ruling Class: The Formation of the Russian Political Order 1700–1825.* New York: Oxford University Press, 1991.

Chapter Five

Crisis and Resolution, 1716–1725

By 1716 Peter had placed much of the government back in the hands of the Russian aristocracy, whether in the Senate, provincial governorships, or the army. The Princes Dolgorukii and their allies had seemed to eclipse Menshikov, but the favorite had made a dramatic comeback over the summer. The flight of Peter's son, Tsarevich Aleksei, created a new situation that ultimately led to the full restoration of Menshikov and the defeat of the aristocrats.

Tsarevich Aleksei had told no one in the government where he was going when he left St. Petersburg, so for the first weeks in Vienna he was undisturbed. On his arrival he had gone straight to the palace of Friedrich Karl, Count von Schönborn, the imperial vice chancellor. In the complex structure of the Holy Roman Empire Schönborn's title signified that he was in charge of the emperor's relations with most of Germany and northern and eastern Europe as well. The count later professed consternation at his late-night visitor, especially when the tsarevich asked for the emperor's protection against his father the tsar. The emperor's council assembled to discuss the issue, and sent an emissary to find out exactly what Aleksei feared and what he wanted. Supposedly Aleksei feared his removal from the succession and for his life as well. What the imperial government decided is not recorded, but they soon moved him and his mistress, Evfrosinia, to the Tirol and then to Naples (for the moment an Austrian possession).

Peter realized that Aleksei was missing in December 1716, shortly before his son's arrival in Vienna. Since Aleksei was the brother-in-law by marriage of the emperor, it was not difficult to guess where he was, and Peter wrote to Vienna. He received only evasive answers, but his ambassador Veselovskii soon was able to find out that the tsarevich was in the Tirol, and Peter sent Alexander Rumiantsev, a captain in the Preobrazhenskii guards, to track him down. Rumiantsev soon learned that Aleksei was in Naples, so Peter wrote again to Karl VI asking permission for his envoy to go and try to convince him to return. The envoy was Petr Tolstoi, former Russian ambassador to Istanbul.

Tolstoi managed to convince Aleksei that his position was untenable and that all he could do was hope that his father would be merciful. By October 1717, he had succeeded and Aleksei set off for Russia with Evfrosinia. As the little party passed through the Habsburg lands, the imperial government made one last try for a different solution. They stopped Tolstoi and Aleksei in Moravia, and back in Vienna the emperor's Privy Conference considered their options. Once again it was Schönborn's voice that was decisive, and unlike earlier discussions, the records of this meeting survive. The vice chancellor argued that Aleksei should be allowed to continue, because he lacked the stability and courage necessary to lead a rebellion against his father. That was the secret agreement that Karl had made with Aleksei. From the point of view of Vienna, it was a perfect scheme, for the Habsburgs feared Peter's growing power in northern Europe, and Aleksei at first seemed to offer them an easy and inexpensive solution.

The tsarevich had tried to enlist not only the emperor's support. During the same summer of 1717 he sent an envoy to Holland to meet with the representative of the king of Sweden, Baron Georg Heinrich von Görtz, who was there on a diplomatic mission. The envoy proposed to Görtz that Charles XII take Aleksei under his protection and Görtz agreed. Unfortunately the Swedish minister had to finalize any agreement with his sovereign, and given slow transportation and the complications of war, he was only able to talk to Charles after several months. The Swedish king was enthusiastic, and Görtz wrote to Aleksei promising him a better army to back him than Vienna could offer, and one much closer to Russia. The Swedish emissary and his letter never reached him, for by that time Aleksei was on his way home.

INVESTIGATION AND TRIAL

The tsarevich arrived in Moscow in January 1718, and right away Peter questioned him about his flight and his intentions. Aleksei admitted, apparently, that he had bragged in Naples that the Holy Roman Emperor would support Aleksei's claim to the Russian throne with arms. This answer not only caused Peter to open a wide-ranging investigation, but also to call the aristocrats, officials, officers, and some part of the people of Moscow to the Kremlin the next Monday. On that day, in front of everyone, Aleksei renounced his claim to the throne in favor of Peter's infant son. Those assembled in the hall signed the proclamation, and Stefan Iavorskii, the metropolitan of Riazan', wept as he signed.

Peter set up an entire new and separate office, the Secret Chancellery under Petr Tolstoi, to investigate the case. Their questions centered on several issues: Who had advised the tsarevich to flee? Who had known that he would flee, and where had he gone? They were not interested in mere opinion, though of course plenty of negative comments about Peter came up in the interrogations. The investigators looked into all of Aleksei's relatives and friends, and quickly found much incriminating evidence involving Peter's ex-wife, Aleksei's mother Evdokiia. It emerged that she had never really become a nun as Peter had ordered her, though she lived in a convent in Suzdal'. She had many conversations with local churchmen who had all sorts of premonitions and dreams of

Peter's demise, and she had also taken on a lover. All this led to a parallel case against her and her circle, but produced no evidence that she or any of her circle was involved in Aleksei's flight. It did show what Peter probably knew already—that there was much discontent among the provincial nobles and clergy.

As far as the flight of the tsarevich went, two men quickly surfaced as Aleksei's confederates. One was Alexander Kikin, the admiralty official convicted of corruption in 1714, who had been actively advising Aleksei to flee, reminding him of the history of the False Dmitrii in Russia and of James Stuart in England and Scotland. Avram Lopukhin, Evdokiia's brother and thus Aleksei's uncle, had known that his nephew was in Austria, and talked about the case with Otto Pleyer, the Habsburg ambassador. Far more important in the Russian elite were P. M. Apraksin and Prince V. V. Dolgorukii. Dolgorukii was one of the first arrested, a tremendous fall from grace for a man only two years before on the verge of ousting Menshikov for the tsar's favor. P. M. Apraksin had been expecting arrest for weeks, and his brother, the Admiral Fyodor Apraksin, had been begging Menshikov to help him. The entreaties seemed to have worked, for Petr Apraksin was arrested early in February, but by March was already out of danger.

The middle of March seemed to bring a quick conclusion to the case. Several of those implicated in the case of Evdokiia were executed for plotting against the life of the tsar. Evdokiia herself was sentenced to prison in the fortress of Schlüsselburg near Petersburg. Aleksei, his mistress Evfrosinia, and several dozen witnesses and prisoners were ordered to follow Peter back to St. Petersburg. On their return Aleksei was placed under house arrest in a building near Peter's palace, and even appeared at some official religious ceremonies. It seemed that the storm might pass.

That was not to be, for some time late in April Peter acquired some new information, most likely from the naive admissions of Evfrosinia, who confessed that in Austria and Italy she had heard from Aleksei that he had many adherents in Russia, in the aristocracy, and in the army, and that it would be easy to overthrow his father. This led to new interrogations of Aleksei under torture, and on May 16 he let everything out, giving a long list of his friends and adherents. He did not charge them with plotting against the tsar, or even with knowledge of his own plans, but he asserted that he had counted on them to support him when he needed them. Aleksei confessed that he had counted on the promises of Karl VI to provide an army.[1] Peter now had a serious dilemma. The interrogations started up again, not only of Aleksei's servants, his household priest, and others, but also of Dolgorukii and various other aristocrats. They confirmed the picture the tsarevich had painted. Peter had either to close up the whole case, making only a few exemplary punishments, or indict much of the Russian elite, and then he would have to punish so many people as would destabilize the state. As the Danish envoy Westphalen put it:

> The number of those who would want that the crown of Russia remain in the line of the eldest prince [Aleksei Petrovich] is so great that it will be necessary that the tsar at last take the part of dissimulation in relation to many people unless he would wish to cut off the heads of all his clergy and his old nobility.

Peter chose the safer course. On Saturday, June 14, 1718, Peter assembled the Senate, the ministers of state, other officers and officials, and the clergy for a church service to pray for aid from the Holy Ghost. Then he took them to the Senate building and announced to them the crimes of his son, producing a box of letters as evidence. Peter asked the clergy and dignitaries to judge him and pronounce sentence. Needless to say, among them were dozens of men implicated by the tsarevich in his depositions.

Three days later, June 17, Peter brought Aleksei before the Senate again. The official report gave only a brief account of

Aleksei's testimony, which appeared very limited in content.
The tsarevich repeated the information that he had given before
and that implicated Avram Lopukhin in contacts with Imperial
Ambassador Pleyer over his flight to Vienna. Then he took aside
Menshikov, Tolstoi, and other dignitaries and told them that
he had counted on people who loved the old ways like Tikhon
Nikitich Streshnev. He had also derived hope from the words
of Prince Vasilii Dolgorukii, who said to him that he was more
clever than his father, that his father was clever, but did not know
people. "You," said Dolgorukii, "will know clever people better." He had always counted on the people [*narod*] and on Metropolitan Stefan Iavorskii after his sermon of 1712. Peter wept,
and again ordered the windows left open and the depositions and
letters of the prisoners read out, with the common people listening in the street. Peter brought Aleksei before the assembly and
announced that his son had violated the oath he swore in Moscow
the previous February to tell the truth, and had planned for a long
time to carry out his plans.

Aleksei then fell at Peter's feet and begged for mercy. When
the tsarevich could stand it no longer he stood up and accused
Peter of ignoring his own flesh and blood, that the tsar had not
brought him up properly as an heir, never considered him the heir,
and raised up lesser men who thought him a fool and a knave. Peter then asked him on whom he had counted, and Aleksei replied,

> The whole country is with me, no one excepted, and I see that for
> you it is a matter of my life, and if you call me a thief, a rogue, and
> a murderer, I want to be one, and I am one and I will gladly die,
> but see what happens to you after my death.

Peter looked at the bishops and said, "Are you not amazed along
with me, and do you not see how stubborn he still is?" Aleksei
seemed to be despairing and Peter took him and kissed him, turning him over to the clergy and the ministers for sentence. Then

the tsarevich returned to his prison, the fortress of Saints Peter and Paul.

Before the sentence was passed, other accused supporters of the tsarevich were interrogated. Aleksei's confessor, Father Iakov Ignat'ev, confessed that the tsarevich had wished for his father's death. This information was damning, but not really new. Prince V. V. Dolgorukii, alone of the men of the ruling elite whom Aleksei had named, was reinterrogated. The Secret Chancellery confronted the tsarevich and Prince Dolgorukii, inquiring about all of Aleksei's statements, including one that Prince V. V. Dolgorukii had been among those "who loved the old ways." The prince admitted that everything Aleksei had said about him was true, except for the statement that Peter did not like clever people. He had not said that. Two days later the prince asked for mercy, alleging that he did in fact tell the tsarevich to send Peter a letter abdicating the succession. After the interrogations Peter was now satisfied of his son's guilt, and on June 22 he ordered Petr Tolstoi to go that day after dinner and ask Aleksei some questions, "not for the investigation, but for knowledge." The questions were very simple: Why had Aleksei disobeyed his father and been so fearless of the consequences of disobedience? Aleksei replied that the origin had been in bad education. As a boy he had stayed with his mother, his tutor Nikifor Viazemskii, and Naryshkin relatives. From them he learned nothing but "peasant games" (*izbnye zabavy*), and by the time his father took him in hand and tried to bring him up as the son of a tsar, he was already spoiled. He could not learn well, and he was already practiced in hypocrisy. Then came Kikin, who merely put in motion what was already there in his soul. His lack of fear came from the same poor character. The rest was understandable. If the emperor had kept his promise to give him an army to overthrow Peter, he would have done it.

On June 24, the day of the last interrogation of Aleksei under torture, the Senate and the assembled officers and officials met to consider the sentence. Six days before the clergy had submitted their completely evasive opinion, concluding that the Old Testament mandated punishment under the law and the New Testament mercy, and it was for others to choose. The grandees made no such evasions. They summarized the evidence for Aleksei's guilt and pronounced the sentence of death, turning the case over to Peter for the final decision. They then signed it, beginning with Menshikov, and then including virtually every person whom Aleksei had named as his supporter (except for the brothers, Princes V. V. and M. V. Dolgorukii, who were still in prison), that is, Streshnev, Musin-Pushkin, Samarin, Prince Iakov Dolgorukii, Petr Apraksin, Gavriil Golovkin, Petr Shafirov,[2] Princes Dmitrii Mikhailovich and Petr Alekseevich Golitsyn, and several Sheremetev relatives of the field marshal, himself absent from the capital.

Peter now had to make a decision to confirm the sentence or not; the clergy and secular officials had recommended mercy. A few more questions were put to Aleksei, mostly to pin down precisely what he had wanted and who were his supporters. He saw his father for the last time on June 26, when Peter went with Menshikov and a number of other high officials to see him in prison. That evening Aleskei's health worsened, and he died that day. The next day, the anniversary of Poltava, the tsar went to church as usual and then celebrated the victory. Aleksei's death had solved the problem.[3]

Essentially the case was over, though the interrogations of Evdokiia's brother Avram Lopukhin continued until fall, when he was executed along with four servants from Aleksei's household. Nothing really new emerged, though Lopukhin did clearly implicate Karl VI's ambassador as a supporter of Aleksei and a conduit of information, leading to a rupture in diplomatic relations between Petersburg and Vienna. Peter was now secure again and moved on.

THE LAST REFORMS

The case of the tsarevich had effects on the whole range of Peter's activity in reforming the government in the last years of his reign. Even before Aleksei's flight, Peter had been contemplating a major shake-up of the structure of government. The establishment of the Senate had provided more coordination over the large provinces, but Russia still lacked an effective central government and a return to the old chancelleries would not do the job. In 1715 Peter hired Heinrich Fick, a Holsteiner who had spent most of his life in Swedish service, to look into possibilities for a reformed administration. Fick proposed the Swedish model, and in 1716 went back to Sweden on a secret mission to acquire copies of the Swedish administrative regulations. His mission was successful, and late in 1717, while Aleksei was still abroad, Peter decreed the establishment of nine colleges, administrative boards to take charge of the various spheres of government activity: justice, finance, war, foreign affairs, and others. The colleges each had eleven members on their governing board, including a president and a vice president who was usually a foreign expert. In the press of business Peter had to delay implementation until after the trial of Aleksei, but ultimately the colleges came into being and lasted throughout the eighteenth century.

The personnel of the colleges reflected the political situation created by the flight of the tsarevich. Most of the presidents were not great aristocrats. The three most prominent were Prince D. M. Golitsyn (Revenue), Prince Iakov Dolgorukii (Audit), and Ivan Musin-Pushkin (Treasury), none of whom lasted long. Dolgorukii died in 1720 and Golitsyn and Musin-Pushkin were removed in 1722. Dolgorukii's office was abolished and the other two went to A. L. Pleshcheev, a simple nobleman without aristocratic pretensions but who had a long career in the army. By 1723 the only aristocrats to head colleges were the Apraksin brothers, Fyodor at the navy as always, and his brother Petr, forgiven for his role in the Aleksei affair, at the College of Justice. In any case the structure of the colleges, where decisions were taken by majority vote of the board, placed a check around the presidents. Most of the presidents were Peter's allies like Menshikov (War) or Golovkin (Foreign Affairs), Russians of lesser gentry origin (Pleshcheev and V. Ia. Novosil'tsev), or generals of foreign ancestry like Adam Weyde and James Bruce. Since all presidents of colleges became ex officio members of the Senate, the Senate was immediately less aristocratic than it had been since shortly after its foundation.

Another victim of the case of the tsarevich was the church, which had been implicated in supporting Aleksei since Stefan Iavorskii's 1712 sermon. Peter had been contemplating changes in the structure of the Orthodox Church for some time, and in August 1718 ordered Feofan Prokopovich, archbishop of Novgorod, to compile a plan for a "Spiritual College" to administer church affairs. Feofan, like Stefan, was a Ukrainian and a product of the Kiev Academy, and had even studied in Rome. Feofan did not take from his Roman training admiration for the Catholic structure, however, quite the opposite, and produced a plan for Russia modeled on the state churches of Lutheran Germany and Scandinavia. The patriarchate was abolished and in its place came the Holy Synod, a board composed of clergy and laymen appointed by the tsar. Its head was a layman, the ober-procuror of the Synod. Thus the tsar could more easily discipline opponents, and also use the church for the educational and welfare tasks that Peter found appropriate. The new regulations also sharply cut down on the number of monasteries, as well as maintaining state control over monastery revenues.

The establishment of the colleges and the Holy Synod were only the first in a long series of measures taken after 1718 that largely created the Russian state structure that lasted until 1801 and in some cases longer. In 1719 Peter broke up the eight large provinces into fifty smaller ones, outlining the duties of each official after the Swedish model, with a provincial governor supported by accountants, bursars, prosecutors, and commissars. In the towns the governors were to appoint a magistracy from among the chief merchants, whose duties were to look after justice and public order and encourage commerce and crafts. At the same time Peter radically reorganized the system of taxation. In place of the old taxes paid by each peasant household, with many complications and extra taxes, he introduced a more or less single tax per male peasant (the "soul" tax). This new form of taxation required a more sophisticated census, so the decrees of 1718 and 1719 were not fully implemented until the end of the reign. The unification of the peasantry and urban poor in one large tax category had implications for later Russian history. It abolished some of the older legal groups in the population, like bond-servants, and introduced a distinction that put serf and state peasants and the urban poor in one group and the gentry and privileged merchants in another. This distinction between the "burdened" (*tiaglye*) and the upper classes, the part of the population exempt from the soul tax, lasted until the Great Reforms of the 1860s.

The Table of Ranks of 1722 introduced equally important changes and distinctions into the legal status of the part of the Russian population exempt from the soul tax. Since Peter had let the old ranking system die starting in the 1690s, the status of the gentry in relationship to service in the army and state had been defined ad hoc. Up until 1713 the clerks kept making the annual lists of boyars, though toward the end they included the new titles, governor, field marshal, general, and others, obviously unsure what to include and what not. The Table of Ranks regularized all this by establishing a civil hierarchy parallel to the military with titles like "secret councilor" taken from German (*Geheimrat*) that put civil officials in a clear relationship to one another. The table also provided a parallel ladder of promotion for both the army and civil administration, and provided that at the lowest rank a man of non-noble origin would acquire personal nobility, and later on, if he went higher, hereditary nobility. A formal way was opened for Peter to supplement his aristocratic officials and generals with talented (or lucky) plebeians. The Table of Ranks lasted until 1856, and in a modified form until the end of the tsarist regime.

Peter's reforms of the last years continued his attempts to reform Russian culture, sponsoring the translation and printing of works not only on architecture, military science, and mathematics, but also on history, on political thought, and even of Western literature in popularized form. In 1724 he established an Academy of Sciences in St. Petersburg, which was supposed to find and support scientists in Europe whose work would be of benefit to Russia and the world. Its task was also to train young Russians in the sciences, and to that end Peter planned a sort of university, a training school to be part of the academy. The academy he founded persists to this day, having outlived the tsars and the Soviets.

Even on the level of daily life, Peter continued to reform Russian life. For the building of the new capital he not only had canals made and palaces and government buildings built, he also issued exemplary designs for houses, forbade building in wood (wood encouraged fires, but the decree was often evaded), and ordered the elite and the merchants to move to the new capital. The new city was constructed entirely on Western architectural models, even many of the churches. The church of Saints Peter and Paul in the fortress was built of brick with a spire like a German Lutheran church, entirely different from Russian tradition with the onion-shaped domes set on a cube-shaped or rectangular building. The city was laid out on a radial plan, the center being not the palace of the tsar but the admiralty. When the French architect Jean-Baptiste Leblond proposed a series of giant squares with a huge statue of Peter as the center of the town, Peter rejected it and sent him off to work on the Peterhof gardens. Peter wanted a rational and civilized city, but not one that simply glorified himself.

A civilized city in the language of the early eighteenth century was one that was "policed," for "police" at that time did not imply repression of crime or dissent as it does today. It was much more. In May 1718 Peter established a police force in St. Petersburg under Anton Devier, a Portuguese-Dutch convert from Judaism.

The new police force, in keeping with European models, included night watchmen on the corners and barriers as checkpoints, with the result that the rampant crime of previous years fell sharply. Devier devoted much more effort to keeping the streets clean, maintaining roads and bridges, and even requiring improvements in buildings that fronted the street. There were elementary attempts to collect garbage, and decrees ordering people to plant trees along the street. A similar force was set up in Moscow.

Similarly by decreeing the existence of new forms of social life, the "assemblies," Peter hoped to introduce refinement and rational ways of passing the time to his countrymen. The 1718 decree cited French practice, and ordered the nobility to put on something between an open house and a ball. In fact he only regulated existing practice, for Western forms of sociability had been common since around 1700. The "assembly" had to include women, a break with the traditional all-male banquets and drinking parties. The amusements were to be more rational than merely drinking and Peter listed cards, dancing, and music as well as smoking, another slap at religious tradition.[4]

Such affairs were not to be restricted to the nobility, for Peter encouraged the hosts to invite well-behaved men and women of other classes. All of these attempts at social engineering, which seem so quaint and unrealistic to modern people, were not attempts to introduce totally new practices: Russians built in stone, planted trees, and had Western-style parties before 1718. What Peter wanted to do was to regulate and universalize the new practices, in keeping with the European ideals of the well-regulated, "policed" state.[5] Like the reforms of government, the move to a more "policed" society gathered considerable speed after the trial and death of Tsarevich Aleksei and the consequent defeat of the Dolgorukii faction at court.

The years after 1718 not only saw formal structures change to a more regularized, law-based, and bureaucratic model, but also saw changes in the informal power structure at court.

Menshikov came back restored to power, if not to the exclusive predominance of earlier years. His rival Prince V. V. Dolgorukii was in exile until 1724, but new favorites emerged, like General P. I. Iaguzhinskii (1683–1736) who received the position of general-procuror of the Senate in 1722. Like Menshikov, Iaguzhinskii was no aristocrat but the son of a church musician from Poland. Iaguzhinskii entered the guards at eighteen, and came to Peter's attention only late in the reign. As in the case of the victorious Naryshkin faction in the 1690s, rivalries erupted among the victors, while the old rivalry of the Golitsyns and Dolgorukiis with Menshikov continued. The most spectacular case was the complaint by G. G. Skorniakov-Pisarev, ober-procuror of the Senate, of mistreatment at the hands of Petr Shafirov and Iaguzhinskii. Skorniakov-Pisarev wrote a letter to Peter in the fall of 1722 on the matter and a few weeks later, the case led to a confrontation in the Senate between Shafirov on one hand and Menshikov and Golovkin on the other. Peter himself was on the coast of the Caspian Sea. The occasion of the confrontation on October 31, 1722, was another case alleging Shafirov's own corruption in the post office, but that was a cover. The real issue was the investigation of Menshikov's illegal appropriation of property around his Ukrainian estate of Pochep, where Shafirov failed to support the favorite. Shafirov shouted at Menshikov that he would not put his head in the noose for him, as Princes Volkonskii and Matvei Gagarin had done.[6] This time Shafirov triumphed, with the backing of Princes D. M. Golitsyn and G. F. Dolgorukii. Shafirov had the support of the princely families in the Senate and Count Andrei Matveev agreed with them in this case.[7] Menshikov had only Golovkin and General James Bruce on his side. When Peter returned, Shafirov and the aristocrats lost: Shafirov was sentenced to death, a sentence that Peter commuted to exile in Novgorod. Punishment fell on Dolgorukii and Golitsyn, and also on Skorniakov-Pisarev. Peter was determined to maintain a balance.

The final years of Peter's reign also saw a major shift in Russia's place in the world. After Charles XII returned to Sweden in 1714 the war continued, though it had been unpopular with the aristocrats from the beginning. They got little, as they saw it, from Petersburg or the Baltic provinces, and their lives seemed to be disrupted just to fight it. In fact, by 1716–18, the continuation of the war was hardly Peter's fault, and the affair of Tsarevich Aleksei kept it going longer. Peter had conquered everything he wanted by 1710, and had even gone on to take Finland in order to force Charles to surrender, but nothing seemed to work. Charles fought on stubbornly, impoverishing his country in the process and only losing more territory. He would not recognize his position and give up. Instead, he spun wild schemes of conquering Norway. He even hoped that if he could make peace with Peter he might be able to persuade the Russian tsar to become his ally! Peter was increasingly frustrated with the war, but could do little but raid the Swedish coast until 1718, when the Swedish Minister Baron Heinrich von Görtz persuaded Charles to negotiate. Then, just as Aleksei sat in the torture chamber, Swedish and Russian diplomats met in the Åland Islands in the Baltic Sea talking peace. Unfortunately for Peter, Aleksei's attempt to solicit Swedish support had undermined Russia's position at the talks. Charles and his ministers believed that a rebellion would break out at any moment in Russia and therefore stalled making any compromise with Peter. At least Charles was willing to think about peace in 1718. When a shot before the Norwegian fort of Fredrikshal killed him in November 1718, chances for immediate peace evaporated because his successors thought they could hold off the Russians with English help. England was a new element in the struggle, for King George I of England was also elector of Hanover and was concerned for his German possessions. The English fleet entered the Baltic to pressure Peter, but no actual fighting with the English ensued. Peter had strong nerves, and he held to his position, raiding the Swedish coast and defeating its remaining navy in a series of engagements. Finally, the new king Frederik I of Sweden sent his diplomats to meet the Russians in Finland, still occupied by Peter's troops. In September 1721, in the town of Nystad, the two sides put an end to the war. Sweden ceded to Russia the Petersburg area, the province of Viborg in southeastern Finland, and the Baltic provinces. The rest of Finland returned to Sweden.

The Nystad treaty confirmed Peter's victories and enormously increased his prestige at home and abroad. At home, the Senate, on the suggestion of Archbishop Feofan Prokopovich, proclaimed him "father of the fatherland," an old Roman title, and emperor. He was now officially not tsar but "imperator," a Latin word imported into Russian. Officially, the Russian tsars held that title until 1917. In Petersburg there were massive celebrations with fireworks, even more magnificent than for the capture of Azov twenty-five years before. Prokopovich and other clergy pronounced orations in praise of the tsar and his victories. Abroad the states of Europe now realized that Russia was more than a regional power on the northeast fringe of Europe. France moved its ambassador to Sweden, Jacques Campredon, to Russia, a recognition that Russia had replaced its rival as the major power in the area. Nearer to Russia Peter had made former enemies and allies into clients. In Poland King Augustus II's disputes with the nobility put the Russian ambassador into the position of arbiter, and Poland was increasingly irrelevant in Eastern Europe and dependent on Russia's good graces. In Sweden the death of Charles XII had produced not only a new king but an elective monarchy where the aristocrats in the Swedish diet held sway. In the Nystad treaty, Peter agreed that Russia would guarantee the new constitution. Swedish "freedom" was a great gift to its neighbors and rivals, and the English and Russian ambassadors spent the next half-century bribing the deputies in the diet to support their governments' policies.

Peace also allowed Peter to look much farther afield. Always interested in promoting Russian trade, he had seen the result of the commercial power of Holland and England, both in the process of building overseas empires that would come to dominate the world. Russia obviously could not compete in that league, but he knew that trade meant wealth. The end of war with Sweden meant that Russia's trade with Western Europe was secure and gradually it shifted from Archangel to St. Petersburg and the new Baltic ports. In the south, Asia beckoned. At the mouth of the Volga by the Caspian Sea, the town of Astrakhan' had become a major emporium, with Indian (Gujarati) and Armenian merchants dominating the trade with Iran and Central Asia. Peter was interested in both areas. Already in 1714–16 he had sent expeditions into Central Asia to explore the area and also the routes that extended on to India. Neither was successful, and the commander of the expedition to Central Asia, Prince Alexander Bekovich-Cherkasskii, a converted Circassian, perished in the Khanate of Khiva. Iran was a bigger prize. In 1715 Peter had sent a young lieutenant, Artemii Volynskii, to Iran not just for diplomacy but to learn more about the land and its products, especially the province of Gilan on the south coast of the Caspian. Volynskii got the information, and in 1719 Peter made him governor of Astrakhan'.

It was Volynskii's repeated reports on the commercial possibilities in Iran that impressed Peter. In addition, Iran under the Safavid shah Sultan Husayn was beset with revolts, in the east from the Afghans and in the Caucasus in Shirvan (central Azerbaidzhan), the center of the Iranian silk industry. It was Shirvan and Gilan that Peter was after. Again with scant consultation of the Russian elite, he brought a large army and a flotilla of ships to Astrakhan' and in the summer of 1722 led them personally south along the western coast of the Caspian. Iran was in no condition to defend itself, and the biggest obstacle was the terrain and, in Gilan itself, the climate. Most of the Russian casualties were from disease. At the same time the Afghan rebels had overthrown the shah and taken power. By 1723, Iran had to surrender and cede to Russia eastern Azerbaidzhan and Gilan. Though it was a comparatively easy victory, the conquest was not a success. The Russians could not cope with the climate in Gilan and the commercial possibilities turned out to be much more limited than Volynskii and others had predicted. After Peter's death his successors abandoned the area and returned it to Iran. Peter was thinking too far ahead. Russia would return a century later to Transcaucasia and even later to Central Asia, but for Peter's time it was too long a reach. The time for commercial imperialism on the Western model had not yet come.

In the very last years of the reign affairs at court became even more tangled, for Peter wanted to secure his legacy. The abiding problem of those years was the succession to the throne. Petr Petrovich died in infancy in 1719, leaving as the only possible heirs Peter's daughters and his grandson Petr, the son of Tsarevich Aleksei. Peter proclaimed in 1722 that the tsar had the right to choose his own successor, but then did not explicitly name anyone as heir. Peter did have his wife Catherine crowned in 1724 as empress, which made it possible for her to succeed Peter on his death. Her principal ally was Menshikov, but he had been under a cloud since 1721 over his Ukrainian estate, and early in 1724 new scandals erupted. Peter was so angry with Menshikov's repeated corruption that he fired him from the College of War and appointed Prince N. I. Repnin, once a client of Menshikov, in his place. Menshikov remained the supreme favorite, but his position was not as secure as in the years 1716–20, and Peter was no longer as close to him personally as he had been early in the reign.

To complicate matters further, Peter betrothed his eldest daughter, Anna, in November 1724 to Karl-Friedrich of Holstein-Gottorp. The marriage treaty specified that she and her husband would have no claims on the Russian throne, but even the announcement of the marriage in June 1723 had given rise to a

"Holstein party" at the Russian court. Karl-Friedrich stayed in St. Petersburg, and as the son-in-law of the tsar did not fail to try to exert his influence, an influence that came to the fore after Peter's death. Since Peter had never proclaimed an heir, when his death came on January 28, 1725, no one knew who would rule the country. In the event, Menshikov and the other grandees agreed on Peter's widow, who took the throne as Catherine I.[8]

POLITICAL THOUGHT

The reign of Peter the Great laid down the foundations of modern Russian culture in political thought, as well as in the arts and sciences. The reception and adaptation of European political thought in those years was a general phenomenon among the Russian elite and characterized both Peter's supporters and his opponents.

The opponents of Peter were not just in favor of different personnel on the throne and in government but different policies as well. Prince V. V. Dolgorukii advocated a return to the "old" ways" and a greater role for the great families, the aristocrats, in the Russian government. This was also the view of one of Aleksei's best-known supporters, Field Marshal B. P. Sheremetev, the commander of Peter's army. Diplomats close to Sheremetev and his family reported that the field marshal wanted to return to the "old laws and religion," to restore the great families to influence, and to ease the tax burdens. Sheremetev, like the other grandees, escaped arrest in 1718, and died early the next year.

The supporters of Aleksei actually had quite a far-reaching set of specific goals as well. They wanted to make peace with Sweden as soon as possible, abandon St. Petersburg, decrease taxes, and dissolve the new European-style regular army. They hated the navy and the presence of many foreigners in the government and military. Since Peter's taxes went mainly to the war with Sweden, the army, and St. Petersburg (Peter lived simply and did not build

huge and grandiose palaces), complaining about the taxes themselves had a political overtone.

Peter was right to think that if his son Aleksei succeeded him
on the throne, his entire legacy was at risk. He and his supporters' ideas, if put into practice, would have meant a sharp halt to
the Europeanization of Russia. Without St. Petersburg, Russia
had no accessible place for permanent contact with Europe, for
in those days only sea transport was relatively easy. Russia could
not expand its trade with Europe for the same reason, so without
the new capital Russia would remain largely outside the rapidly
developing networks of world trade. The new army was the key to
the conquest and maintenance of St. Petersburg, exposed as it was
on the northwestern fringe of the country. The new army also required a new sort of service to the tsar from the nobility, one that
was more extensive but also one that did not guarantee high positions just on the basis of birth. Though Peter kept aristocrats like
Sheremetev in the highest commands, he expected expertise from
his fighting generals. None of the reforms, military and civil, was
possible without the presence of foreign experts with knowledge
that the Russians were only in the process of acquiring. This was
true of engineering projects like the canals and the draining of
marshes on the Neva, of administrative reforms like the colleges,
and of the new-style army. All these innovations required higher
taxes, though the main drain on the country was naturally the war
with Sweden.

The opposition to Peter that the affair of Aleksei revealed was
not merely a transitory phenomenon. It was the first appearance
of a conservative, aristocratic ideology that persisted in Russia
throughout the eighteenth century. Its most famous exponent,
Prince M. M. Shcherbatov (1733–90), believed that Peter's reforms had brought about the moral degeneration of the country
because of its exposure to alien values. The result was despotism,
the rule of women, and corruption. Shcherbatov preached a return to an aristocratic government, which he found in the reign

of Aleksei Mikhailovich, a form of rule that had never existed in fact. Only such an aristocratic government, which freed the aristocrats and maintained serfdom, could successfully rule Russia.

Shcherbatov may have been the most skillful exponent of these views, but he was not the first. Prince Boris Kurakin (1676–1727), from 1711 to his death one of Peter's premier diplomats, had already worked out most of the conception. The prince was one of several young men whom Peter sent in 1697 to Venice to study navigation. He did some of that but mostly Kurakin acquired a Venetian mistress and good Italian, which allowed him to read the history of Venice and its constitution. He concluded (wrongly) that Venice was in decline because its oldest aristocracy of warriors and landholders could not keep out the new money, but that in its prime the Venetian aristocracy had been cultured and effective. Fascinated by the aristocratic Venetian republic, Kurakin's political ideas were completely Western. His unpublished manuscript history of Peter's reign claimed that Peter had continuously neglected and repressed the aristocratic families since 1694 and vilified all of Peter's supporters and close friends. This notion was a wild exaggeration, but it served as an argument for the virtues of aristocracy. Kurakin kept all this to himself, for his first wife was Tsaritsa Evdokiia's sister, making him Peter's brother-in-law, and he served the tsar faithfully as a diplomat. Despite his faithful service, he saw the world very differently from his master.

Kurakin died soon after Peter, but other aristocrats from Peter's time lived on and tried in 1730 to put these ideas into practice. When Tsarevich Aleksei's son, Tsar Peter II, suddenly died in 1730 and Anna Ivanovna, Peter's niece, came to the throne, some of the grandees tried to impose a constitution on her that would give power to a Supreme Privy Council composed of aristocrats. Unfortunately for them they were too greedy: In fact the Golitsyn and Dolgorukii families would hold all the power. The leaders of this attempt had been Peter's grandees and generals, Princes D. M.

and M. M. Golitsyn and the remaining Princes Dolgorukii, including V. V. Dolgorukii, Peter's erstwhile favorite exiled in 1718–24. They lacked support among the elite at large, including other aristocrats, and were soon overthrown. Aristocratic conservatism remained a potent stream of thought, but it was a minority faith.

The conservatives who opposed Peter were not single-mindedly anti-Western. Sheremetev, as we have seen, was so interested in Catholicism that he almost converted, and he was a man of largely Western culture. Prince D. M. Golitsyn had an extensive library of Western books and was close to the Ukrainian churchmen of Kiev with their largely Polish culture. Kurakin wrote his pleas for aristocracy in a language that was literally stuffed with Italian phrases, idealized the Venetian past, and bragged about his Venetian mistress. Aleksei Petrovich himself read and spoke German, went to French comedies in Dresden, and also had an extensive library of Western books. He exchanged books with Prince D. M. Golitsyn and the Ukrainian clergy. None of these men were narrow xenophobes: They looked to different aspects of the West than Peter did. The conservatives, generally speaking, looked to Poland, to traditions of aristocracy and oligarchy farther west as in Venice, and cultivated a vision of society that stressed ancient families and their value. They were fascinated by southern Europe and some with Catholicism.

Peter and his supporters, like the diplomat Count Andrei Artamonovich Matveev, the son of Aleksei's favorite, took a different direction. For them the main social value was order, which they saw as something achieved by rational action of the state. Matveev's history of Peter, in contrast to Kurakin's, stressed the disorder that resulted from the revolts of the musketeers and the involvement of Sofia and the Miloslavskiis in these revolts. The message was that great noblemen should not try to undermine the tsar by allying with plebeian or other rebels, for that led to social and political chaos. Matveev and other supporters of Peter saw his accomplishments less as "progress," as later generations would, than as the imposition of order on a chaotic society. They also saw Peter's encouragement of European culture as the bringing of the arts and sciences (not just "Europe") to a backward, ignorant country. While the conservatives saw religion as an ally, Peter and his men saw it as necessary but not in political affairs. The task of the church was to civilize the people, not to instruct the tsar.

If Matveev was a good example of the notions of the typical nobleman who supported Peter, Archbishop Feofan Prokopovich took a more sophisticated line that reflected the degree to which Western political thought influenced the Russian intellectual elite. His 1722 tract in favor of sovereignty and Peter's right to choose his successor, the *Justice of the Monarch's Will,* was entirely cast in the terms of the rationalism and legalism of seventeenth-century Europe. To make his case he cited the Dutch jurist Hugo Grotius (1583–1645) to buttress Peter's claims to choose his own successor to the throne. For Grotius natural law was the foundation of the state, and all states, monarchies or republics, possessed sovereignty. Feofan drew the conclusion that a sovereign ruler could pick his own successor. Feofan followed his Western models in analyzing the nature of the state, not Orthodox tradition. Feofan's tract was worlds away from the religious notions of tsardom that had held sway in Russia for the previous centuries.

Just as the conservative and aristocratic line of thought continued after Peter's death, so did the notions of order and learning that characterized the tsar and his supporters. With the evolution of political thought in the West, the emphasis shifted from regulation to enlightenment and rational reform. In Russia as elsewhere, a powerful stream of Enlightenment political thought saw the best engine of reform in a powerful monarchy, which could, it was believed, rise above the narrow interests of the various groups of the population. Later Russian exponents of this idea, like the scientist Mikhail Lomonosov (1711–65); the satirical writer, journalist, and freemason Nikolai Novikov (1744–1818); or Catherine the

Great herself (ruled 1762–96) took inspiration from Peter and the type of political thinking that he and his followers exemplified. In their minds reason, not local custom or privilege, should be the basis of the state's policies. Russia had become part of Europe culturally under Peter, and in their minds this was an unparalleled benefit, for to them Europeanization meant not the substitution of one culture for another but the spread of knowledge and universal values of justice and progress.

Peter himself, in personality and cultural tastes, was more complicated than his supporters. His whole life went to reinforcing his monarchical authority as tsar, but abroad he was most comfortable in the Dutch Republic. He preferred sea captains to courtiers, lived in a modest house (much less grand than Menshikov's), and liked to work with his hands. His normal dress was ordinary, even a bit shabby, except for rare state occasions. Physically he was nearly seven feet tall, towering over all contemporaries, but also rather thin, with narrow shoulders. His hair was very dark, almost black, as were the moustaches he wore rather than a beard. He was a man of great endurance and fairly robust health. He could drink considerable quantities of vodka (though he actually preferred Hungarian wine, presumably Tokaj) and stay up long hours, but he was not free of disease. He suffered repeatedly and seriously from "colic," apparently some sort of stomach or intestinal disorder, but it was a urinary tract infection that eventually killed him.

Peter preferred Dutch architecture over French grandness because the Dutch were good at drainage and made better gardens. Dutch was his preferred foreign language, though he could manage in German. He was not particularly interested in the literary and historical culture of the West, which Kurakin and Matveev craved, and preferred architecture and engineering. He had some rudimentary idea of European science, and in England he wanted to see mathematicians and boatbuilders. Nevertheless he supervised the translation into Russian of European works in pedagogy, history, and politics as well as those in architecture or fortification. When the fancy took him he even interfered in the details of translation. Peter had no theoretical ideas about government of his own, but he came to prefer rationalist political theorists like Samuel Pufendorf (1632–94), whose history of Europe appeared in Russian translation. Shortly before his death, Peter also ordered Pufendorf's more popular account of government, *On the Duty of Man and Citizen according to the Natural Law*, to be translated into Russian. Pufendorf did not advocate a particular form of government, but he did provide a description and analysis of the state based on natural law and the social contract.

Peter has the reputation of indifference to religion, even of hostility to Orthodoxy, but this reputation lacks foundation. He was certainly more than a little critical of the clergy, for what he saw as the excesses of monasticism, the church's opposition to his policies, and its meddling in politics. At the same time his attendance at liturgy was frequent if not daily (as the older practice of the court had been), and he knew his sacred history. His letters and reported conversations have numerous biblical references and quotations. Personally he was interested in both Catholicism and Protestant religions, and decreed that they both be tolerated in Russia. In England he attended Quaker meetings and seems to have met William Penn. At the same time his policies maintained Orthodoxy against its Russian opponents and critics. The Old Believers were not arrested, but they had to pay double taxation.

No puritan, Peter was enraged by the corruption of his officials, including Menshikov, and he had no hesitation about expressing it, even if he knew he needed them too much to fire them. He saw himself as a tutor of European manners to the Russian elite. One of the Danish diplomats reported that he used his court dwarfs to teach the boyars European manners, for they were allowed to mock the great if they kept to the old manners. If the boyar who had been subject to this treatment mended his ways, Peter gave him a wooden drinking cup made by his own hands on his lathe.

Peter was often happiest in a military camp with his soldiers. There he lived in a simple tent, the sort issued to captains, and went about the army with no suite and no guards. His other and greatest love was boats. On his birthday he sometimes took the court and the ambassadors out on his personal yacht, a gift of William III of England. Once he went out in high wind, and sailed about the Gulf of Finland while so drunk that the Danish ambassador feared for his life. Drunken carousing and his beloved fireworks were a regular feature of Peter's celebrations. He was so uncomfortable with the old Russian court rituals that he let them disappear, but he took more than a decade to begin to import European etiquette. Even then, he avoided such ceremonies personally whenever he could. He divorced his noble wife and took up eventually with a Livonian servant girl, whom he married and made his empress and successor, Catherine I. None of this behavior reflected values shared with the Russian aristocracy, even with his supporters. His behavior did reflect a strong and independent personality with the political skill to transform his country's culture and state.

NOTES

1. Peter never found out about the attempt to enlist Sweden on the side of Aleksei.

2. Gavriil Ivanovich Golovkin (1660–1734) came from a lesser noble family who entered first the household of Tsaritsa Natalia, then of Peter himself as chamber *stol'nik* and then as head chamberlain (*postel'nichii*). He headed the Ambassadorial Office, and later College of Foreign Affairs (1718), receiving the title of chancellor (1709). Petr Pavlovich Shafirov (1669–1739) was the son of a converted Jew who served as a translator in the Ambassadorial Office and accompanied Peter on the trip to Europe in 1697. He served as Fyodor Golovin's private secretary from 1703, worked under Golovkin as vice chancellor from 1709 to 1723. After 1725 he served primarily in the College of Commerce. The two carried out the planning and execution of much

of Peter's foreign policy. Most observers believed that it was Shafirov who was the more able and knowledgeable and with a better command of foreign languages, and that Golovkin frequently simply followed his lead. Both of them remained largely independent of the court factions, cultivating Menshikov in the early years of his power, but by 1715 turning toward enmity without joining his opponents.

3. Naturally rumors immediately spread that he was murdered, presumably on Peter's orders or with his connivance. The official announcement was that he had died of an "apoplexy," normally interpreted as a stroke. Actually, no reliable evidence exists to determine how he died. He certainly had been in poor health for years and the torture sessions, while neither frequent nor unusually horrific, must have been harmful. All the murder stories were rumors, some of them from sources forged in the nineteenth century. The only honest answer to the dilemma is that no conclusion is possible: The sources we have permit no conclusion.

4. The Russian church had opposed tobacco in the seventeenth century not for health reasons but on the grounds that it was Satanic. Perhaps they meant that it was fun.

5. Peter did not have anything like a modern "police" force, much less a "police state" in the modern sense. Besides the night watchmen in the two capitals, there was no professional group to fight crime or dissent. Political matters came to the government's attention only when there were rebellions or other acts of defiance like the flight of Aleksei, or from denunciations from the population. The government investigated such denunciations in the Preobrazhenskii Chancellery, a court, not a police force. The Secret Chancellery set up in 1718 to investigate Tsarevich Aleksei lasted until the end of Peter's reign and beyond, but had no greater staff than the Preobrazhenskii Chancellery. Peter had no network of paid informers who listened to tavern gossip and passed it to the government, as was the case in France under Louis XIV. Russia was too backward for such a system.

6. Both Prince M. I. Volkonskii and Prince Gagarin had been executed for corruption.

7. Count Andrei Artamonovich Matveev (1666–1728) was the son of Artamon Matveev, the last favorite of Tsar Aleksei. A man of wide education, with a good knowledge of Latin and French, he served Peter as ambassador to Holland (1699–1712), simultaneously taking care of

Russia's relations with Great Britain and France. After a brief appointment in Vienna (1712–15), he returned to Russia to serve in a variety of administrative capacities. He remained outside the court factions but was a firm adherent of Peter's power and an opponent of the aristocrats. He reflected these views in his manuscript history of the events of 1682–98, on which see below.

8. Catherine lived only until 1727, and on her death Petr Alekseevich, the son of the unfortunate Aleksei Petrovich, took the throne as Peter II. Menshikov went into exile in Siberia, from which he never returned. Peter II was increasingly under the influence of the Golitsyn and Dolgorukii families and the court returned to Moscow. On his sudden death in 1730 Peter's niece, Anna Ivanovna, succeeded him and exiled the Golitsyns and Dolgorukiis. This was their last attempt at power in Russia.

FURTHER READING

Bushkovitch, Paul. "Political Ideology in the Reign of Peter I: Feofan Prokopovich, Succession to the Throne and the West," in ГИИМ: Доклады по истории 18 и 19 вв. DHI Moskau: Vorträge zum 18. und 19. Jahrhundert. http://www.perspectivia.net/content/publikationen/vortraege-moskau/bushkovitch_ideology.

———. "Power and the Historian: The Case of Tsarevich Aleksei, 1716–1718, and N. G. Ustrialov, 1845–1859," *Proceedings of the American Philosophical Society* 141, no. 2 (June 1997): 177–212.

Cracraft, James. *The Church Reform of Peter the Great*. Stanford, CA: Stanford University Press, 1971.

Meehan-Waters, Brenda. *Autocracy and Aristocracy: The Russian Service Elite of 1730*. New Brunswick, NJ: Rutgers University Press, 1982.

Peterson, Claes. *Peter the Great's Administrative and Judicial Reforms: Swedish Antecedents and the Process of Reception*. Skrifter utgivna av Insitutet för rättshistorisk forskning 29, Stockholm, 1979.

Raeff, Marc. *The Well-Ordered Police State: Social and Institutional Change through Law in the Germanies and Russia, 1600–1800*. New Haven, CT: Yale University Press, 1983.

Chapter Six

Monarchy, Aristocracy, and Reform

The problem of Peter's reign was that the informal structures of power were not in the tsar's favor, nor were they in favor of the process of reform. The traditional role of the boyar aristocracy in Russia meant that any attempt at reforming state and society on the part of the tsar had to take the great families into account. Yet despite the aristocrats' incipient cultural Westernization, most of them were opposed to Peter's policy. Indeed early in the reign it seemed that he alone was the guarantee of success of any sort. The Danish envoy Heins summed up in 1699:

> If God gives his grace to the Tsar to live a considerable time more, it is clear that he will put Muscovy on a footing such as it has never been on before. It is also true that this prince risks a great deal, and that human fatality (which Heaven forbid) would be capable of putting everything to rout, and into a state more deplorable than this country has ever been, because of the disunity of minds and the jealousy that exists among the boyars and among all the people.

Virtually everything Peter did brought complaints in high quarters, the war, the new-style army and navy, the new dress, St. Petersburg, higher taxes for the war and for the new capital.

Yet the aristocrats never overthrew him. They did not take advantage of Charles XII's advance into Russia in 1708, as the Swedish king was sure they would. They sympathized with Tsarevich

Aleksei in 1716–18, and might have gone over to his side if he ever really did return home at the head of a foreign army, but they were not going to move on their own. There seem to be two reasons for their apparent inaction. One was that they were not the archaic xenophobes occasionally depicted in popular fiction. Rather, they were almost as Westernized as Peter, although with different tastes in European culture than the tsar himself. Another reason was that Peter was, after all, the legitimate tsar. This fact made Charles XII's hopes of rebellion illusory, but also made Tsarevich Aleksei a potentially serious threat. In normal times, it meant that Peter could walk about without guards or suite and fear nothing, for the aura of majesty was too great. And on a more practical level, any disturbance of the political order might have unimaginable consequences, as the boyars saw in the Time of Troubles and more recently in 1682. Finally, Peter knew how to compromise by putting the aristocrats back into government with the new provincial governorships and the Senate. When the case of the tsarevich told him that they were not trustworthy, he did not try to imitate Ivan the Terrible and execute them en masse; he merely failed to appoint them to most of the new colleges, clearing central government of most aristocrats but leaving them as provincial governors and military commanders.

All these factors merely mitigated Peter's difficulties; they did not remove the basic fact that the Russian elite was not favorable to his concrete measures of reform. Complicating the sullen opposition of the great families were their mutual rivalries, which enraged Peter as early as 1698. His first solution to both sides of the problem, to bypass the aristocracy and thus wholly reorganize Russian government, was a response to the attitudes of the elite. This policy did not work, for the tasks of government were too complex, and the problems he had set out to solve remained. The aristocrats still opposed him, and the lack of order in the administration of the country only grew worse. Peter responded by the establishment of the big *gubernias* in 1707–8 and by the establishment of the Senate three years later. Peter's appointments to the governorships and his appointments to the Senate restored the aristocrats to the center of power and simultaneously provided a more orderly government. The favorite Menshikov, even before his fall from grace in 1714, came to be surrounded by powerful dignitaries of impeccably aristocratic origin.

Their new positions did not diminish the hostility of the aristocrats to Peter's reforms. His new favorite, Prince V. V. Dolgorukii, helped increase the power of his own family, Peter's opponents, and it was the Dolgorukiis who benefited the most from Menshikov's eclipse in 1714–16. The case of Tsarevich Aleksei only made Peter even more aware of the extent of opposition to his reforms among the elite. Peter responded to that opposition, and to the rivalries of the great families with one another and with Menshikov, by once again reorganizing the state. Beginning as early as 1715, he laid the foundations for the colleges, which were to introduce a regularized system of administration in which trained experts and experienced noble administrators had more voice than the grandees. From 1718 he altered the character of the Senate by including the college presidents, most of whom were not aristocrats. He broke up the big *gubernias*, and put in charge of them some aristocrats, but many more officers and administrators who were surely noblemen, but not great aristocrats. Peter needed new institutions and loyal, capable men to staff them. He could only find them in the requisite numbers outside the boyar aristocracy, and only with such men could he be sure of success. At the same time, reliance on non-aristocratic ministers exacerbated the discontent of the old families. The paradox is that the opposition of the aristocracy throughout the reign served as a continuous spur to reform, forcing Peter to search for new institutions and new men. Perhaps a lesser monarch might have just given up in exhaustion, but Peter never faltered. In the end the victory was his.

Primary Sources

DIPLOMATS AND TRAVELERS

de Bruyn, Cornelis. *Travels into Muscovy, Persia, and Part of the East Indies*, 2 vols. 1737, Eighteenth Century Collections Online.

Perry, John. *The State of Russia under the Present Czar*. 1716, Google Books.

von Strahlenberg, Philip Johann. *An Historico-geographical Description of the North and Eastern Parts of Europe and Asia: but more particularly of Russia, Siberia, and Great Tartary*. London, 1738. Google Books, Hathi Trust.

Weber, F. C. *Present State of Russia*, 2 vols. 1722–23, Eighteenth Century Collections Online.

Whitworth, Charles Lord. *Account of Russia as it was in 1710*. Strawberry Hill, 1758, Eighteenth Century Collections Online.

PETER'S SPOKESMEN

Cracraft, James, ed. *For God and Peter the Great: The Works of Thomas Consett, 1723–1729*. 1982 Reprint of contemporary translations of the *Spiritual Regulation*, some other works of Feofan Prokopovich, and documents on the Persian campaign.

Prokopovich, Feofan. Orations on Peter the Great in Marc Raeff, *Russian Intellectual History*, 1966, 13–20; and Harold Segel, *Literature of Eighteenth Century Russia,* 1967, vol. 1, 141–48.

———. *Justice of the Monarch's Will* in Anthony Lentin ed. and trans., *Peter the Great: His Law on Imperial Succession: The Official Commentary*, Oxford, 1996.

Shafirov, P. P. *Discourse Concerning the Just Causes of the War between Sweden and Russia, 1700–1721*, Dobbs Ferry, NY, 1973.

THE OFFICIAL RECORD OF
A CRUCIAL MOMENT

The Tryal of the Czarewitz, Alexis Petrowitz, who was condemn'd at Petersbourg, on the 25th of June, 1718, for a design of rebellion and treason against the life of the czar his father. Written originally in Russian, and publish'd by order of His Czarian Majesty, and now translated into English. London, J. Crokatt, 1725. (various reprints and online at Gale, Making of Modern Law).

A UNIQUE DOCUMENT

Fedosov, Dmitry, ed., *Diary of Patrick Gordon of Auchleuchries 1635–1699*, Aberdeen, 2013–16, vols. 4–6. The diary of a Scottish mercenary officer in the Russian army, a favorite of Peter the Great in the 1680s and 1690s.

THE VISUAL RECORD

Shvidkovsky, Dmitri. *St. Petersburg: Architecture of the Tsars*; photographs by Alexander Orloff; New York, 1996.

Index

Index

About the Author

Paul Bushkovitch was educated at Harvard College and Columbia University. He is the author of *The Merchants of Moscow (1580–1650)* (1980), *Religion and Society in Russia: The Sixteenth and Seventeenth Centuries* (1992), *Peter the Great: The Struggle for Power, 1671–1725* (2001), on which the present work is based, and *A Concise History of Russia* (2012). He is Reuben Post Halleck Professor of History at Yale University, where he has taught since 1975.